AF594130

A Seven Year Lifetime:
Discovering Life in the Face of Death

by David Carrier

ISBN 978-1-63393-292-0

Published by

köehlerbooks™

210 60th Street
Virginia Beach, VA 23451
800-435-4811
www.koehlerbooks.com

A Seven Year Lifetime

a true story

Discovering Life in the Face of Death

DAVID CARRIER

VIRGINIA BEACH
CAPE CHARLES

To Nancy, who taught me life was not measured in years but in moments–moments of crystal clear connection that love has to offer when I'm willing to accept it.

Introduction

As you read this book you will find entries from a journal I kept to read to Nancy. The entries are placed at the beginning of the first seventeen chapters. Except for these inserts the book is in the order of events as they happened. At the time of writing the journal she was unconscious. I wasn't sure how long she would be in that condition or even if she would survive. This was my way of telling her what happened to her, and how I felt. These journal entries took place years after we met, and though the book is otherwise in chronological order, they serve a purpose.

In chapter seventeen and eighteen the book is no longer in two different time sequences. This is where the past and the present meet. I placed these journal entries there because the fear of death is almost always near the surface of a patient with a terminal illness. They serve as a reminder that after you've gotten the news and you feel fine, and things look good, or even promising, the thought of death always lingers in the shadows. It's there to give the reader a sense of what it was like for us, starting each day with, "I'm glad to be alive, but I wonder if I'll be dead later."

I used the dates to show when these events took place. The days, the hours, and the minutes were what mattered to me most at those times. I refused to miss a moment with Nancy by being distracted by thoughts of the past or the future. When Nancy and I put the thoughts of death aside, the question then became; how much can we live before we die.

Foreword

All of us have a terminal condition. It's called life, and it ends. So how can a life that ends in death have a happy ending? Live differently, live with passion, and embrace every moment.

In these pages you will find extraordinary life. You will find love that supports without question and without question of having it returned. This is the true story of what some would call a life that was cruelly cut short, but in truth, those seven years we shared was a full lifetime of complete majesty. Given the chance, Nancy and I would do it all again: Even if we couldn't change a thing.

Chapter 1

I speak to Nancy, even though she can't hear.

Sunday May 6, 2012, 6:00 a.m.

I *was awakened early when you invaded my sleeping space. I asked if you were okay, you seemed to nod and you helped me as I repositioned you to your normal sleeping position. I tried to get back to sleep. I could hear your rhythmic breathing, so much louder with the air forcing its way around the tumor near the back of your tongue. This didn't keep me up; as a matter of fact, I couldn't rest without hearing it.*

Your alarm went off at 7:00, as usual. The normal morning routine would be for the alarm to beep progressively louder for several minutes before you would snooze it. For some reason I was not in the mood, so I got up, noticing your position was now more drooped than usual. Something was wrong. I called your name, louder than normal. "Nancy," I said. "Are you okay?" No response. "NANCY," I yelled, louder this time; no response.

I dialed 911, the whole time talking to you and the operator at the same time as I was hurriedly getting dressed. You were still breathing but completely unresponsive. For the first time since I first heard you had cancer, I thought you might really die.

NANCY'S STORY

More than once in her younger days Nancy had been dragged out of a pool hall by her hair for hustling. She had a sense of adventure, and liked to see how far she could go. And isn't that what college is about? As time went on and she began to feel the need to settle into what most of us would call a normal life, she fell in love and decided to marry. Like many before her, it was a poor choice for both her and her husband. She married a man who got so drunk on their wedding day that he had to be held up to participate in the ceremony.

It could be at that time they *were* made for each other, but I didn't know her back then. They separated some time later and Nancy decided to divorce him. She told me they went to couples counseling and when the counselor asked him about what he wanted out of their relationship he told the counselor he'd do anything it took to get them back together. When the counselor asked Nancy what she wanted she said, "I want him to QUIT CALLING ME." For her, the marriage had been over almost before it began.

Nancy had a degree from Temple University and a good job supervising engineers who built airplanes. She studied several spiritual practices and became certified in hypnosis and proficient in meditation, yoga, and Reiki, which is a spiritual practice for stress reduction and healing. She attended spiritual retreats, joined a Religious Science church, which teaches that God is everywhere and that the best way to understand God is to find God within yourself. She began studying to become a Practitioner in the church.

She even went skydiving, something many people may put on their bucket list, but very few actually go through with it. She met life head on, and knew with the beginning of each day, a whole new life was ahead of her.

I never met the young Nancy who got dragged out of bars by

women twice her size. The Nancy I knew was intelligent sweet, elegant, and spiritual. They say every saint has a past, and every sinner a future. That could be written about her. When she finally reached a place where she felt completely empowered, worthy, and ready for anything, something changed for her. That something would give her a completely new outlook; not just on her life, but on life itself.

Nancy was ill. In pure scientific terms, she had terminal adenoid cystic carcinoma, a kind of throat/neck cancer. This was not a secret, although I did not know the intimate details of her condition at that time.

Later, she told me the pain started about six years before we got involved, in the year 2000. She had a sore throat that wouldn't go away. She went to the doctor after trying a lot of over the counter medications that didn't help. Over the next few years, X-rays were taken, blood was tested, levels were checked, Nancy was poked, prodded, and examined in all ways possible to discover the cause of her discomfort, but with little positive results. After Nancy found a lump on the right side of her throat in 2002, a biopsy was ordered. The results were good news: negative. No cancer, yet the pain continued.

In 2004 the doctor(s) ordered another biopsy. This second biopsy revealed cancer. Apparently, the first attempt had missed the tumor. The tumor was on the salivary gland; it was approximately 5mm in size. They called it Adenoid Cystic Carcinoma (ACC). All those syllables can take some of the feeling out of it, but there was no place for her to hide.

Even after living it alongside the woman I loved, I still can't imagine what it would be like to be told I had cancer. For me, it would be like being told my expiration date. Most people live into their 70s or 80s.Yet we are not told in our early 60s that we only have about 10 to 20 years to live. We are not told that as we age we will lose our ability to do things like eat what we want, sleep without pain, go to the bathroom, or even smell the flowers. We are not told we will lose mobility and independence. But when they occur gradually over time we accept these things because we are near the end of a lifetime.

Do we put off living because we feel we will live forever? Do we believe we are immortal until someone we hold in authority tells us our time here is coming to an end? I don't know. I do know that for me if I were thirty, sixty, or even ninety, it would be too soon to hear that cancer would be my end. For me, old age is the only acceptable way to die; anything else would be robbing me of precious time. I would have squandered that time had I not known Nancy.

At first Nancy took the news of her diagnosis pretty hard. She had been eating very healthily by the standards of the day and felt betrayed by her body. She told me she spent the two weeks after the diagnosis eating primarily French fries, as she came to grips with her condition. She shared very little of how she was feeling with her family or friends, keeping most of her feelings to herself.

She expressed to me a sense of failure combined with regret and anger, each taking its turn at ruling her mood until the overwhelming sense of being a victim took over. But Nancy was a master at hiding what was going on under the surface. She would act poised and appear to have everything under control, and then she would prepare to get her treatment options into focus.

After seeing the foremost specialist on ACC she was told that her only option was to have radiation followed by surgery. They said there was a chance they could get out all of the cancer. Of course, there was no guarantee without surgery to see clearly what was there. With the removal of the tumor she would likely suffer nerve damage, as this type of cancer grows along the nerve pathways. She was also told that after the surgery she would most likely be unable to swallow or speak.

Nancy decided that living like that, with the possibility that this would not get rid of the cancer, was not an option she was willing to pursue. She instead chose a holistic alternative. Her treatment involved organic raw foods, prayer, chiropractic, acupuncture, massage, and Reiki. With these treatments in place over the next two years, she took her belief in herself to a new level. She decided that she could have all she ever wanted: being free of cancer, buying a home, and finding the love of her life.

In 2006, two years after Nancy began her alternative treatment, she was given a CAT scan. The nurse told her that the results revealed that the tumor had not grown in the last two years. This gave her the hope she needed to know that all was going in her favor. Her pain level had remained steady and she felt she was making progress with her treatment choice. She had a positive team she believed in, and who believed in her as well. It was truly the fight of her life.

Not too long after this she joined with two of her friends to form a prayer circle. There were still two things missing from her treatment requirements. First, she wanted a home of her own. She was making this purchase so that she could have space in her world for the second missing piece.

She wanted to be married to a man she could love and trust, and who would love her beyond measure. She wanted someone who would not be scared of the fact that she had cancer. She was looking for the kind of man who would use all his being to keep her in the light and not let her fall into darkness, no matter how the appearance of her body might change. She created a space for her new love, although she didn't know who he was. She did know she was looking for her Hero.

How hard would you work toward doing everything you ever wanted to do if you knew your expiration date? What if the thing you wanted most was a partner to share all the things you always wanted to do with? How difficult would you believe it to be to find someone and have him stay in your life after he heard you had a terminal disease? How difficult is it to live our lives without one?

MY STORY

I had just ended a nine-year marriage in 2006. I ended it because I believed I was inconsequential in the lives of my wife and stepchildren. In many ways that was true. After the towers fell on September 11, 2001, the president said that every individual who died in the towers was the most important person in someone's life. I realized if I had died in those towers, his statement would be false. You see, I felt that I wasn't even the most important person in my own life.

With that realization, I decided that I *was* important. I knew that nothing was going to change in my marital relationship without help. My wife and I had no partnership. We lived separate lives that happened to run parallel to each other. In the years before 9/11 we went to a counselor. At first I think there was a genuine desire to change our relationship. After a full year of trying several counselors, it became evident that neither of us had the willingness or ability to do what it would take to heal our differences.

It would be easy for me to blame the woman I couldn't get along with for the slow demise of our relationship but no marriage ends without both parties contributing. It took a long time for me to have the courage to accept that neither of us would compromise. The one thing we did agree upon however was the importance of her children, whom I loved very much. I believe we did an honorable job in holding our relationship in a good place for their sakes.

We continued with our conflicts unresolved for years after that, neither of us willing to step away from a familiar, yet emotionally unfulfilling union. Somehow I thought that staying over those last few years was better than being completely honest, and just asking for a divorce. Today I feel differently. I should have been honest with her about wanting to end the relationship. At the same time, I am glad that we stayed together until her youngest was graduated and married. In 2006, when her little girl was grown and gone, it was time for me to leave.

About that time my friend Mike needed someone to house sit. It was the perfect situation for me. I could move out of the house of the woman I drove crazy, and not experience the usual expense of having a security deposit, and last month's rent. I knew it would be temporary but it bought me some time; time that I would use to figure out what I wanted.

In the past, whenever a relationship ended I would go on an immediate search for a new one. Not this time. I would start out with the intention of being alone, and being patient. I wanted to find someone who could be everything I wanted in a rich, loving partnership that shared common lifetime goals, but I also knew I wasn't ready yet.

I started by answering one simple question in earnest. What did I want in this amazing new relationship? The answer came to me immediately. I wanted to be the most important person in someone's life. I wanted to completely immerse myself into her life, (not in the creepy way, but in the devotional sense) and I wanted her to do the same with me. I wanted us to share things that are hard to share and be honest about the little things as well as the big things.

I wanted this woman I had yet to know, to be elegant and feminine, yet strong and willful. I wanted her to be deeply spiritual, and able to make a commitment. I did not want a girlfriend; I wanted a life partner. Another thing I realized was I needed to know what I was willing to offer.

Every man wants to be a knight in shining armor, to save the day. Men dream about this as children. Little boys ask themselves, "Is being a superhero too much to ask?" When someone asked me what superhero I wanted to be I said, "Santa Clause. He is loved by all, is very generous, works magic, and is never bothered by the cold. Also he is very forgiving. No matter how things go throughout the year every child seems to make the nice list."

The truth is I was willing to give everything, but like all the love I had experienced, and maybe the love most of us know, I wanted it to be appreciated. That meant that the love I offered was a conditional love. It was less than the idea of perfect love I knew to be true, but it was the best I could do at the time.

Nancy and I had known each other for ten years as members of the same church, but we had never really made personal contact. I have read and observed that when we look at something only a small portion of what we see is in focus. In essence, the rest of the vision goes largely unnoticed. This was how it was with us, neither was the focus of the other's attention.

At that time, Nancy and I were attending classes at our church to become licensed practitioners. This is someone who is licensed by the church who is trained to listen and pray for the congregants. Practitioners also lead meditations and in some cases teach Religious Science or other classes. Before we can do any of this however, we take a few years to get rid of our own baggage. In our case we were both trying to find a way to let go of our past. Our hearts were broken and raw, yet we were open to possibility. Our time was about to begin. We were finally ready.

A home improvement contractor by profession, I was teaching a ballroom dance class during this time in our lives. I had already taught several and Nancy had attended them all. She followed my lead beautifully. With the slightest inclination she would move at the same speed as me in any direction I wished for her to go. We moved as one, and when she was in my arms we were one. I never had this experience dancing with anyone before in my life. But even with all this apparent demonstration of our compatibility, we did not act; I out of a sense of obligation to wait more time before seeing someone, and her out of respect for my healing. In other words, we were chicken.

It is said that to live a free and happy life we must sacrifice boredom. This is not always easy. Many of us get into a lifestyle that feels comfortable and begin to settle. Settle down, that's what they call it. It's when you put away the childishness, and accept the way life is. We were both tired of settling. It wasn't working for either of us. We knew there was something more. What we didn't know was how close we were to finding it.

Chapter 2

Sunday May 6, 2012, 7:07 a.m.

"I want to wait till the last minute to get the tracheotomy." I was remembering your words as I waited for the 911 operator to tell me the ambulance was in route. I just hoped that this wouldn't be the last minute of your life because you waited too long.

OUR TRUE CONNECTION–2006

A woman at church I called Mom asked me about a dance routine. I called her Mom because when we first met, she said, "I'm not sure what happened that you weren't born into my family, but I'm pretty sure you're my son." As my mom had died when I was seven, I took advantage of her offer. Truth be told, she knew me better than my real mom. Mom reminded me, I wanted to do this routine in the 1980s but never got the chance. She suggested that perhaps Nancy would be a wise choice for a dance partner. "She would," I replied.

"You should ask her," she said. "You two dance so beautifully together I can't imagine it wouldn't be everything you wanted."

I could feel her handprints all over my back. I wondered if she was pushing Nancy too, Secretly, I hoped so.

It took another week for me to muster up the nerve to ask

Nancy about helping me. She said yes with a quiet confidence I had yet to see in her. There was no fear. It startled me a little, although I'm not sure what I expected. We started staying after class each week to work on the dance.

After a few weeks we decided to try going to a studio dance party to try out our dancing skills on a real dance floor. It was then I realized how much dancing had changed since I first became an instructor. My confidence was fading faster than red undies in a load of bleached whites in hot water. It was obvious I needed to rethink the plan.

The plan was to woo Nancy into seeing what a wonderful talented man I was. I wanted to demonstrate that I was more than just a carpenter. I was a man of the world, intelligent, confident, sophisticated, and witty; so we could take our relationship to the next level. It wasn't much but...well... sometimes a plan seems more foolproof in my head than it does in real life. It never dawned on me that it may have been a fool who came up with the plan.

When we went to the dance I did the unthinkable, that is, I stopped thinking about the dance. I asked her to go on a real date with me. I can't remember my words but I'm sure they were clumsy and awkward. It had been over ten years since I had asked anyone on a date, and Nancy was so different from anyone I had ever met. We were both in what most would call middle age, but this felt as exciting as if we had been teenagers.

Taking a relationship from friendship to something more was bigger to me than anyone ever led me to believe. It's very easy to walk on a sidewalk. It's wide enough to have several people pass each other in several directions; but imagine placing the sidewalk a thousand feet in the air with no handrails and suddenly it seems very narrow. The sidewalk has not changed, but fear has been introduced.

Asking Nancy out on a date was a simple task, but the question had the potential to end a friendship, even one as long as ours.

Whatever I said, she just listened and looked at me with a smile, "I would like that," she said.

The happy dance was in my near future. Time went from a crawl to a sprint by the day of our date. I understood that when

I felt confident it was like I could put the sidewalk back on the ground. But as I prepared for our dinner date I was once again high in the clouds, this time, unable to even see the ground.

We decided on a restaurant that was close to her house. It was elegant without being overstated, served wonderful Italian food, and had been there for years although it had gone largely unnoticed... it was just like Nancy. I was nervous and scared as I drove up to her house. She was so elegant, smart, attractive, and everything desirable. It felt as though if I didn't amaze her with my dashing appearance, witty charm, and overall manliness, I would be dismissed as quickly and unceremoniously as a Russian fish packer running for congress. With time running out, I headed toward her door.

I wondered what I would say that could make up for the deficit I felt between us; with nowhere to go but up, I decided on honesty. I knew there would be no faking anything with Nancy. I stood on the step raising my hand to announce my presence when she opened the door.

I could feel a bit of panic sweeping over me as we exchanged hellos, and a quick hug. I figured the less I said at this point the better, but she just took my arm and smiled at me. I knew I was either being pardoned, or set up for the slaughter. I was cautious as we walked to my truck, and as I opened her door she said, "Thank you, you look really nice tonight."

A wave of relief swept over me as I walked around to my side and slid into the driver's seat. "You look stunning," I said, as I started the truck and backed out of the driveway.

Nancy was wearing a brown dress she said she had purchased for this date. She told me it was the only one that fit her slender frame the way she wanted. I realized a few weeks later when I shopped with Nancy for the first time that getting that dress must have taken hours, in at least four stores, over several days, possibly in several cities or even states. She would not have made this decision until she had all the possible options presented to her. At the time I thought, this dress is beautiful, and I can't believe this beautiful, elegant woman is going to dinner with me.

I made reservations the day before our date, and when we arrived at the restaurant we were seated quickly at our outside table. The temperatures were in the mid-seventies, the sun was on its way down, and I got the feeling that all of nature was smiling at us.

As we dined I noticed how when she sipped her water; she always held it in her mouth just a little before swallowing it. I didn't mention anything but I did wonder about it. This was the first thing I had noticed that reminded me of her condition. Until that time, I had not given it a thought. I asked myself if I thought this would make a difference. The answer was a resounding NO. First of all, I believed she could easily beat cancer, and second of all I believed with all my heart and soul that I could help her if that's what it took. It was easy to push this concern from my thoughts.

The dinner went on with good food and enchanting conversation about absolutely nothing, and I was just lost in her beauty, a beauty that seemed to shine from within. It was like we decided to use the time to observe each other rather than impress one another. Aside from the way she swallowed water there was no trace of illness in her that I could clearly identify.

She was perfect just the way she was, and I knew in my heart we could share a lifetime together. I knew that while she was with me there would be nothing I would need but her to sustain me. I understood that together we were so much more than the sum of the two of us. Together we created our own universe, our own planet; our own lives lived as one. Everything I ever wanted was in that moment. The only thing we couldn't do was make the moment last forever, instead we would cherish the memory.

At the end of our date I told her how pleased I was about how things had progressed between us. She reflected the same sentiment then cautioned me with a statement that we lived by for the rest of our time together. "No matter how good things get," she said, "they can always be better."

In ballroom dancing a partnership is formed. The man leads, and choreographs the dance on the fly. The woman follows and through her movements adds grace and beauty to the dance. While in dance frame, where the couple is holding each other the woman may sometimes rest her arm on the arm of the leader. My dance teacher told us in a class, "Ladies you must hold up your own weight. If you let your arm relax then the man's arm gets tired and the frame collapses. Then the lead/follow process disintegrates. Remember you're a partner, not a passenger."

In my past relationships one or both of us had always let the framework of our partnership collapse. We lost our ability to communicate our intentions. With Nancy, for the first time in my life I felt like I was in a partnership where we were both completely committed to the dance. The best part was, "Things can get even better."

From there our romance blossomed from the passion of the first infatuation to a deep love of each other. We learned the little things and got all the usual important issues discussed. Things like, do you like to watch basketball, and I hope your favorite football team is the Cowboys. These were *her* important considerations. She was a much bigger sports fan than me, and while it might be okay for me to like the Patriots, I was never allowed to cheer for them, especially if they were playing the Cowboys. In exchange for my hometown loyalty, she would do things for me that no one else had ever considered. We would set aside time to talk of what we wanted as well as what we feared. We planned trips together and we took them.

She showed me that I was just as important to her as she was to me. We talked of our preferences and took each other's needs into consideration, and as with any partnership, when she asked me for something, she asked me what she could do so that I could give her what she requested. I told her it wasn't so much about the material gifts as the memories. I told her the thing I held most valuable was time: If she could spend more time with me that would be the greatest gift she could give me, and in return, there was nothing that I would not willingly give to her.

My birthday approached not long after we had that talk, and as with all new couples she asked what I would like for my birthday. In keeping with our previous discussion I told her it would be wonderful to just spend the day together, and maybe have a cake. I could see by the look on her face that asking was more a formality than anything else. She already knew in that engineer mind of hers that she was going to top any birthday I ever had.

She was going to hit a homerun with the bases loaded three runs down in the bottom of the ninth at the World Series, score a touchdown in the final seconds of the Super Bowl, and make the three-point shot at the buzzer to win the NBA Championship. She was going to do something so spectacular that I would spend the rest of our years trying to do anything that would just come close.

Five days before my birthday I was informed that my present had arrived. She was giving me a birthday week. Each evening for the next five days I would receive something to celebrate my birthday. The first night I got a wonderful meal prepared just for me at her home. She served dinner to me in courses while she asked me about my day and listened intently to every word I spoke. It was all about me. The second day, she took me shopping to buy me some new pants and a shirt that I would need later in the week. On the third day she took me to get an ice cream cake. On the fourth day she took me to the movies. These were all things that I deeply enjoyed.

I couldn't imagine what the last day would bring, but from what I knew of her, it was going to be something I would not soon forget. I was instructed to wear my new clothes. On this night I was taken to downtown Fort Worth where we had dinner at one of the finer dining establishments. I was given a new watch, as a reminder of her recognizing that time was important to me. When we finished I was taken to the Bass Performance Hall to see one of my favorite singers perform an incredible concert. When the concert was over, the applause died down, and the seats were mostly emptied, I received the greatest gift of all. She took my hands, looked deep into my eyes and said, "I Love you Honey Bunny, Happy Birthday."

In that moment I knew that even though I would continue to get older, I would never need another birthday. I made a silent vow to give her every day, as long as we were together, the gift of letting her know she was cared for, respected, honored, and loved to the full extent of my abilities. I felt in my heart that to fail, even one day, would be unacceptable. It would dishonor what she had so unselfishly begun. She set the standard higher than anyone I had known. It was now up to me to be equal to her commitment. I would make up for in length, what she had given me in height.

After that I set my sights on keeping our relationship moving forward. It was time to boldly go into that place where we start taking about the future. If you have cancer it can be a scary talk. If you have a past it can be a scary talk also. I knew I was willing to bet on Nancy. I wondered if she felt the same about me.

Chapter 3

Sunday May 6, 2012, 7:09 a.m.

I *remained on the line with the 911 operator until EMS arrived. It took them less than five minutes to get to the house. I showed them in and explained your condition. They contacted the hospital and relayed the information I gave them while I quickly got ready to go. Soon we were on our way.*

Upon arriving I gave your information to Dr. Weston, who would be treating you. "Nancy is a stage 4 cancer patient with tumors along her salivary glands on the right side of her throat. Her airway has been partially obstructed for some time, but she wanted to wait to have a tracheotomy. The tumors may make giving her a breathing tube difficult."

"Nancy's condition is very serious," said Dr. Weston, "does she have a DNR (Do not resuscitate) on file?"

"No" I said, "Nancy told me that when the time came I'd know what to do."

"If her condition deteriorates further what would you like us to do?"

A NEW LIFE FOR US BEGINS

If you want to live a free and happy life, don't you think you need to know what a free and happy life is, at least to you?

What do you want for supper, your birthday, Christmas, your anniversary? What movie would you like to see? What kind of clothes do you want? What do you want to get at the grocery store? Where would you like to live? If something happens to you, what would you like me to do?

Questions like these are asked every day, and for me the answer is usually I don't know, or I haven't thought about it. They don't seem that important. But Nancy's cancer forced us to accept that our time together might be cut short. What would you do if you had six months, six weeks, or six days to live? With this in mind go back and ask those questions again. After you answer, ask one more; what are you waiting for? Start living right now. Look all around. That's life going on. Remember, you're a participant in life, not a passenger.

The next six months of our courtship were a whirlwind of activity. My work was keeping me very busy and when I wasn't working I was finding time to be with Nancy. It was delicious to experience so much. Each day was filled with life in both activity and quiet, measured passion. Our senses were alive with stimulation. It was as if the world around us suddenly went from black and white to color. Of course I knew the same could be said of many relationships, but the degree to which it happened for us was new.

Nancy had signed up for the Life Directions seminar as part of a package at the first T. Harv Eker Peak Potentials event we had attended together. His seminars taught how an individual could learn about and reach their full abilities. I signed up about a month after we started seeing each other after I found out she was going.

Attending this seminar together, we learned our talents, our preferences, what gives us joy, and how to survive a plane crash in the ocean with a small raft. We were all looking for something to work toward that would give our life meaning, or at least direction. For Nancy and me it was learning and teaching. We each could look at our lives and see the events as adventures that taught us lessons. We considered our experiences as the classroom of life.

The right teacher made learning fun, but a poor teacher made difficult concepts even harder to understand. Having this insight we decided to set our focus not just on being in the school of life, but being each other's teachers.

We flew to L.A. together and got our room at the hotel, beginning our Life Directions event. On the second day of the seminar we listened to a song that we were asked to take to heart. This song was about finding out that you were dying. I looked at Nancy and saw she was crying. I motioned for one of the volunteers to come over with a box of tissues. I knew at once I was in big trouble.

When the song about dying ended Nancy said, "Don't ever let my experience take you out of your experience. We are both here to learn, and if we continue to be distracted by each other we'll never get anything out of this. Please promise me you'll be present to your own feelings." Nancy was asking me not to lose myself even if her cancer progressed. She loved me enough to want me to maintain some focus on my own needs.

"I will, I promise."

After that, we found we could learn some things best by separating for a brief time into other groups, and then meet up afterward and compare notes on how each of us felt about whatever subject was being addressed. It was interesting how being apart to discover our own experiences allowed us to be closer when we returned to each other. We both had our own lives to live, but we also wanted to spend as much of our time together as we could.

On the last day of the event there were always opportunities to purchase another seminar for a discounted price that was only available that day. We knew how this worked, and we were ready for a purchase if it was something that we felt would be beneficial. The event being offered was called Extreme Health. It would have presenters from many different fields focusing on healthy living. This sounded like something right up Nancy's alley. For some reason I felt no urge to make this purchase.

I looked at Nancy and said, "Honey, I'm not sure why but I don't feel like I'm supposed to sign up for this today. What are your feelings about it?" She gave this some thought, and said, "I don't think you are either, but I don't know why."

We decided to just sign her up at that time, like when we went into different groups to learn our own lessons, and then later we could come together to share. We would discover why this needed to happen soon enough.

When the event ended, and we returned home we felt we were on our way to something special. We were both interested in the same type of future. We were also interested in having a future together. We decided to take things to the next level. It was time to meet each other's families.

Chapter 4

Sunday May 6, 2012, 7:14 a.m.

"What do you want us to do Mr. Carrier?"

I actually never thought I would be asked this question. I figured they would just keep working on you as long as the DNR was not in place. Now I was being asked a question that I could not answer. At some level I remembered what you had said to me about not wanting to go on if you couldn't eat the things you liked, and speak to those you loved. I also remembered what I said about being able to make only one choice. It was my choice to make. Should I let your suffering end or let you endure more pain with little hope for change just because I am completely and totally selfish?

MEETING NANCY'S FAMILY

Nancy's family lived here in Texas. My first experience meeting them was at a Christmas party. There were over fifty people there; it turned out to be a surprise party as well. She said she had a big family but I had no idea I would be meeting them all at once. "Surprise." It seemed like each and every one of them had something to say to me, or ask about who I was, or what are my prospects, or what are my intentions, etc. I definitely got the third degree, and several death threats that I considered the *first* degree. There was one man, Nancy told me, that I needed to meet. He was the patriarch of the family, and his name was Ennis.

In all the forgiveness classes I have taught or attended, the one group that comes up without exception as a target for forgiveness is family. Whenever anyone gets into a committed relationship they do so with their partner's whole family. The opportunity for forgiveness can double in the blink of an eye.

The first time I saw him all I could think of was the movie, *The Godfather*. The family waited in line to see him and ask advice. They did everything but kiss his hand. I was tempted but decided this was too sissy for Texas.

When it was time for me to see him I was notified that my presence was required. I dutifully approached knowing all eyes were upon me. He asked if I knew who he was and I told him I did. He then asked me a few questions that I cannot remember. All I recall is watching his lips move and feeling my lips move, words coming out, and him smiling. Then he shook his head, and I was dismissed. I was still alive and he seemed pleased with me. I thanked him and backed away holding his gaze, like one who might be leaving a lion's den with the pride leader waiting for me to do something silly like turn my back.

Nancy told me later that her family really looked out for her. I believed it. Nancy had dated for many years without having any lasting relationships. I'm not sure why, but I like to believe it was because she was waiting for me. Now I was thinking perhaps they had met her family.

I was never so grateful for taking Life Directions as I was that night. The time that Nancy and I had spent in separate groups taught me to trust that she was okay, and pay attention to what I had to do. If I had been too connected to her at the party I'm pretty sure the family would have seen it as I was looking to her to save me from them. As it was, I made a good impression, and they showed me much more respect than I could have hoped for. Nancy was very proud of me, and let's face it, to me, that's what mattered most.

After the party we talked about the experience in the same way we shared things after being in separate groups at Life Directions. She told me I made a good impression and some of them even said, "He's a keeper." Of course that would only matter if Nancy agreed.

"I agree with them," she said.

"I always wanted to be a kept man," I said.

She smiled at that; melting my heart the way only she could. I knew as long as she was in my life, my life's direction, purpose, and goal would be to make sure I never gave her any reason to question how I felt about her, and that she would always know, she was my whole world.

I have noticed that many, like me tend to paint a darker picture of their own family than is accurate. Nancy's description of her family was accurate; they were hard working, intelligent and close. After I described my siblings, Nancy thought she was meeting the Addams Family.

In the summer it was her turn to meet my family. Nancy was going to New York State for a seminar called "Wizard" We would fly up there; I would rent a car, and drop her off at the event. I would then go to visit my family in New Hampshire for three days until she finished, then go pick her up. We would then go to northern Maine to go whitewater rafting with my whole family. As it turned out, there were a lot of people going, and Nancy would get to meet almost seventy of them all at once. Ha, ha, ha...I have a big family, too.

Things went as planned with dropping Nancy off, and my going to visit the family. I made sure they understood to be on their best behavior and let them know how important Nancy was to me. They were very excited to meet her. The few days flew by and I was soon on my way back to pick her up.

I arrived at Wizard camp at about eight a.m. as was requested of me. When Nancy was not ready at 8:30 I went to the desk to see where she was. They gave me her room number and headed down the hall to check her room. It had already been cleaned. This made me a bit nervous. I returned to the desk to make sure I had the right room and they assured me it was. I began calling her cell phone over and over trying to get through. I had no success.

On my next trip to the front desk I asked if anyone was left from the Wizard group. They said there were about fifteen people who had not checked out. At this point I let them know that Nancy was a cancer patient and was supposed to meet me thirty minutes ago and was not answering her cell. We knocked on three doors before we woke her up from a very sound sleep in a room where she had been reassigned. As it turned out she had the room to herself, and had turned off her cell.

I am a positive-thinking person, but words cannot describe how scared I was. I could not imagine what might have happened to her. I knew there were hundreds of others at the retreat and thoughts of her wandering off, getting lost, being abducted, having some health-related emergency with no one to help, all raced through my mind. She was mostly punctual, prepared, and always planned ahead. I knew she wouldn't be ready to go, I knew that, but she would be almost ready. Finding her flooded me with joy and fear: Joy, knowing she was okay, and fear wondering if this is what it would it be like in the end if I lost her to cancer. Does knowing where she is make so much difference? Only if she said she would be there. That was the difference. If I believed she was where she wanted to be it didn't matter. What mattered was having every minute I could with her.

Filled with relief, we shared a long hug, and I helped her pack. We stopped to have some breakfast on the way out. Over breakfast she told me that they were once again selling Extreme Health, and if you bought a ticket you could take two friends. She told them she had already purchased the tickets at the Life Directions retreat and they said, "Well then you can take two friends with you to Extreme Health for free."

We looked at each other smiling for a long time. As we walked out to the car I asked, "Can I be one of your two friends?"

"I already put your name in," she said.

After that, we headed to northern Maine to a place that was far, far, far off the beaten path. Nancy said she wanted to see a moose. I said, "Me too, a chocolate mousse."

There was no cell phone service within an hour of the campground where we were staying. It was the first time in about eight years that I didn't have a phone stuck to my hip and it was wonderful. We would take the next three days and focus on the beauty around us. We had the opportunity to forget about doctors, cancer, schedules, appointments, and work. All we needed was each other and a raft. There was no TV and I think only one radio station.

Before rafting, we had a day of floating the river below the rapids. On that day we watched an eagle circle, swoop down and try to catch a fish. It missed on the first run but came back around and caught it the second time. It was an unplanned event that we were able to share together. We marveled at how we could be so far away from all the everyday forms of entertainment, and find something that was common, even ordinary to this river that we would never forget.

How amazing it is to watch such an event in person. We had both seen similar scenes on TV yet neither of us could remember even one of them. Still, what just happened would be part of us forever because it was shared. It was real life happening before our eyes. We wondered what else life had in store for us. We were anxious to devour all that was available because together, everything seemed to double in value. A feeling of joyous overwhelming was all around us, but the scariest challenge was just ahead of us. It had nothing to do with water; it was all about the fire, the campfire.

That evening we sat around the campfire and talked and joked, and had a good old-fashioned campfire experience. It was the perfect place for the family to get to know Nancy.

I've found that campfires evoke stories of our past, plans of our future, and the most embarrassing moments of our lives–some of which happen at the campfire. The first questions were about how we met. This was followed by Nancy talking a little about her work at a company that builds airplane wings. She explained how she was in charge of fasteners, nuts and bolts, and things like that.

At first we could tell how this work seemed trivial to everyone, but when she explained the stress on the wings and what would happen if any fastener should fail, people quickly understood how important her job was, and how much stress she placed on herself each day. She had been at this job for about thirty years, manufacturing the same wing.

My sister El was thoroughly impressed with Nancy. She could fit in and still not lose sight of who she was. Nancy was a city girl but fit in with my country family the same way she fit in with her own. She knew the mannerisms and what was important to them. She could get along with almost everyone, and like me, she knew whom to impress. In my family there were two: my sister El was the matriarch and my brother Norman was the patriarch. They both had equal power and influence, and both would be impressed with Nancy's ability to give as good as she got when it came to playful teasing. Norman was pretty easygoing and took warmly to Nancy. El was all about how Nancy treated me. She could see that even though Nancy had her health challenges she was an expert caregiver and automatically looked after me even as I was doing all I could to take care of her.

Of course once Nancy had been accepted, my role as the caregiver was first in El's mind. Nancy could see how my sister always looked after us. El made sure we had privacy even in the crowd of family that surrounded us. El would look after us both and do what she could to keep us safe. Nancy accepted her care with gratitude and appreciation. She thanked her for her efforts and noticed every kindness.

Nancy had walked through the campfire untouched by the flames, yet warmed us all with her presence and light. Later my family told me, "She's a keeper."

I replied, "She spreads life wherever she goes."

WHITEWATER RAFTING

On rafting day, we had to cross over into Canada to get into the river. We were told that beginners should get into a ten-person raft and experienced rafters should use the six-person rafts. Because the ten-person rafts were bigger and heavier, they were a little smoother through the whitewater than the smaller six, also with more people, if one of the rowers was weak or tired it didn't make as much difference. The guide could still keep the raft under control with the other eight or nine rowers.

Nancy told me to get a ten for us and hold her place while she made a trip to the restroom. Then she left. I found a six right away and secured a spot for the two of us not saying a word to the guide. I knew at that time Nancy had gone skydiving. I knew she had climbed to the top of a sixty-foot pole, climbed on top of that pole, stood up, jumped off, and grabbed a flag. The pole was only twelve inches in diameter. To understand this, just imagine yourself climbing up the outside of a six-story building looking down to find you are standing on a platform the size of an old record album. You are then encouraged to jump up and grab a flag above you. She was courageous beyond measure. The excitement of the six-person raft seemed right for us, and there was a good chance we would never do this again. It was easy to make the decision.

When Nancy got back she was surprised at my decision and expressed a little concern. The guide heard us then asked everyone in the raft how much experience we all had. As it turned out, out of six, three of us had no experience rafting. She said we could practice on the land and if we could listen to instructions, and follow the directions quickly, and correctly we could remain in her raft, but one slip on land and she would ship (pun intended) us off to another group. Everyone on that raft stepped up and performed flawlessly. We took ownership of our raft and made our guide proud.

When we set the raft into the water we were pleased to discover that the river was warm. This was because a small distance up river was a power plant. Being from Texas, we were grateful, as we were not used to the cold temperatures up North. We were instructed that after the raft was in the water we would be rowing across to the other bank and holding position until we were cleared to go downstream. We performed as instructed and again earned the praise of our guide who informed us of the dangers of the next section of the river. She told us that we could go through a safe section or go through what they called Maytag, because it was like trying to navigate a toy boat in a washing machine. Of course we went for Maytag.

We were immediately pushed from side to side, frantically paddling as our guide shouted instructions, telling us what direction and with how much effort we should pull. We were a well-oiled machine that was being tossed about like a wet rag doll in a front-loading washer, and we thoroughly enjoyed the ride. As we exited the rapids, I glanced at Nancy and she was smiling from ear to ear. So was I. The six-person raft was the right decision. Our accomplishments were stored in our memories and the experience spoke loud and clear. Today we met life on our own terms, and lived fully for our efforts, but things can always be better.

All Nancy could say about Maytag was that it didn't last long enough. We both agreed it was one of the most exciting things we had experienced, at least up to that point. Time went quickly on the river and soon all the groups were ready for a rest. In a calm section we stopped for lunch and were informed that the last rapids were just down river and they were called the floating rapids because we could jump out of the raft and float through the rapids, then get back in the raft a little downstream. If we chose to do this, our instructions were to keep our noses and toes in the air at all times, and breathe in as we came up out of the water. She also said to try to relax as best you can.

Of course Nancy and I went for it. This experience was like getting eight big glasses of water for the day in about one and one half minutes. Nancy did much better as it took her almost three minutes to get her eight glasses of water. After we climbed back into the raft exhausted, and gasping for air, we went to our places and grabbed our paddles. We looked at each other and realized we were both smiling. It was a revelation in our relationship. We would try new things together and trust each other to be safe. We both knew our own limits and had a pretty good idea of the caution areas of each other. In short, we were growing closer while trusting each other apart, and it felt right.

As we continued our journey, the thought of losing sight of Nancy in the floating rapids did not bother me. I knew some of that was because I was trying to survive myself, but after the incident at the hotel, I was concerned that I might be too protective. I wanted her to live the life she most wanted on her own terms. That day, I realized that there was a strong possibility that I could do it, at least as long as I didn't lose sight of her for more than a few minutes.

After rafting we were exhausted, but the family was going on a hike to a waterfall in the woods. The path was down the road from the campground. Could we stand to see one more of nature's magnificent wonders? The answer was yes. The hike turned out to be about a mile but it was definitely worth it. The falls dropped about 150 feet and there were places along the bank where there were decks set up with railings for safety.

Nancy ignored these and climbed out onto a rock outcropping to get the best view and take in the full impact of the falls with the sound of the water roaring in her ears. She sat there for about fifteen minutes just lost in the powerful energy flowing eagerly by just below her. I would not have been so calm sitting at the edge like that, but she seemed completely at peace.

When we finished there and were on the way back to camp, I asked her about her experience sitting out there near the edge of the falls. She told me that being out there was where she felt closest to God. There on that ledge she felt like she had her own life in her hands, and by getting up and going back to the trail she would choose life. It was a decision she felt she had to make often, always knowing that it was her choice. Her life would be her choice, not cancer's or any other disease. It wasn't in the hands of a doctor or medical institution, or even me. She made the choice many times every day, to live.

As I looked back across the days we spent there, I saw that the events for the most part could not have been planned. We chose wonder and awe for our intended experience and left the rest up to Spirit. Our experiences had brought both Nancy and me to a place of choosing life in all its magnificence. She would continue making that choice throughout our time together. This would not be limited to sitting on cliffs or riding the rapids, life would give her opportunities to live through much more than she could have imagined at that time. Yet no matter what the choice entailed, she always found a way to say yes to life.

Chapter 5

Sunday May 6, 2012, 7:15 a.m.

"Do what you can to keep her with us," I said, feeling my selfishness begin to overwhelm me. I was pretty sure I would not regret my selfish decision, but I wasn't sure that you would say the same. One moment later, your heart stopped.

"I will need you to stay outside the room while we work on your wife, Mr. Carrier."

I had known for some time that you would not die with me in the room. I froze in my tracks with what felt like the sounds of a freight train running through my head. Dr. Weston said it again, "Please wait outside Mr. Carrier," this time louder and in a way that let me know it was in your best interest to do it now.

MOVING OUT AND MOVING IN–2007

Nancy had been looking for a house for some time, although I did not know this. One night after a shared dinner she asked if I would like to go for a drive. I agreed and we headed south toward a lake that was nearby. She told me that she had been looking for a place on the other side of the lake.

As relationships grow, life has set up many challenges for each couple to move through in order to learn to work together, get along under duress, and learn to compromise as both their preferences are revealed. It sounds so easy, and it might even be fun. I could see the little cartoon birdies and little beating hearts floating in the air around us as little animated forest animals played happy music in the background.

She said she chose it for two reasons. "One, I wanted a place that had room for a new partner in my life, and two, I wanted a place where my new partner wouldn't have to spend time fixing it up. This house is only five years old, and according to the inspector it's in great shape."

I considered this to be very thoughtful on her part. That, or she had no confidence in my ability to remodel, even though I had a successful business in just that. Either way I win.

"Well I guess the least I could do, would be to help you pay for it," I replied.

In many relationships that progress, there comes a time when both parties decide to cohabitate. With us that happened about six months after we began dating. Although I had space in the new house that was designated as "mine," there would be additional space needed, as I was giving up my apartment. The events that led up to our sharing a home set the tone for the rest of our relationship.

THE MOVE

The first thing was to get Nancy moved into the new place. It went something like this.

I said, "When movers come in I think they go room by room packing everything in the room onto the truck, before going onto the next room."

After I said this I began to pack a box.

"Wait a minute," she said. "This is how I like to pack. First I pick something up and hold it in my hand. I consider whether or not I will need it, or even want it. Only then can I put it in a box or in the trash. That way I don't take anything I don't want."

Although I could understand the efficiency of the process with regard to not moving excess items, it sure put a time issue on the people I had lined up to help Nancy move on this particular day. I was pretty sure I would have to let them go home until we had gone through the whole house. This could take a week, and the fact was we had to be out of that house in two days. I found my calm being challenged.

"Nancy," I said, "I have friends coming over to help us get stuff to the new house, and we only have a day or so to get things out and have this place cleaned up. I'm a little concerned with the time line. What do you think?"

Nancy gave a deep sigh.

"I was just considering that," she said.

That was it, no fighting, no arguing, just working together. It felt great.

With her permission our friends and I then began packing up the old place, and getting things to the new home. I have to say that Nancy did better than I expected as she only stopped us a few times to consider whether something should be moved or thrown away. We finished with time to spare. In the new place the ritual of what to keep and what to discard was resumed, but this time with the added advantage of seeing how the old items would fit in the new home. Almost nothing was thrown out, and somehow what remained took up more space than it had at the old place. I thought to myself, "This is going to make my move easy. Since there's no room for any of my stuff, all I have to do is give it all away."

Our new home was a three-bedroom brick house with vaulted high ceilings, two full bathrooms, a formal dining room, a formal and informal living area, a fireplace, and a two-car garage in a beautiful neighborhood near a lake. It was less than five years old, and didn't need a thing done to it. Now add in the fact that this was a serious relationship that will most likely lead to marriage, and that I am a high-level remodeler. Little did I know Nancy had a plan for everything, and that plan would both amaze and delight me in ways I could not have predicted.

My remodeling and cabinetry skills were well known to Nancy and although she had chosen our house based partially on the idea that it didn't need any immediate repairs that did not mean that things could not be improved.

"No matter how good things are they can always be better," she said.

I discovered this in an experiential way, on a trip to an electronics store I'll call, "All Things Expensive" or ATE for short. It started one evening when she asked me if I would mind going shopping with her. I agreed and asked, "Where would you like to go?"

She said, "Let's go to ATE."

This seemed curious to me, but being a guy with a chance to go to an electronics store, what could I say? When we arrived she looked around and went directly to the big screen high definition TVs. She found one that was set up in a mock living room with a sofa, chairs, and surround sound. She sat on the sofa and I sat beside her. We watched as an action movie played on the big screen with a picture so clear you could read the menu in the wall of the restaurant that was about to be blown up. She put her arm around me and snuggled close. She asked, "Is this the size TV that would be appropriate for our living room?"

With exuberant excitement I replied, "Why yes, Honey, it sure is."

She laid her head on my shoulder, with her arms around me squeezing me tight, and said, "As soon you build me some built-in bookcases and entertainment center on either side of the fireplace mantle, we're going to get one of these."

I have to admit at that point the only response I could come up with was to laugh out loud.

She was brilliant. She went through a complete negotiation with me, including closing the sale, and I didn't even know I was involved until I was willing to give her everything she wanted. Of course, this would not be the last time that she would get her way by getting me to agree to do what she wanted, without her having to ask. Nancy knew me very well.

Not long after this incident Nancy's friend Linda was moving to Hawaii. Linda decided to sell her bedroom set, and high-definition TV as well the surround sound that went with it. As it turned out we were in a position to buy. I assured Nancy I would not even unpack the TV until the bookcases were built. But we'll get back to that.

We changed out our bedroom set with the newly purchased pieces and added an eight- drawer dresser that we purchased from a fine furniture store. It closely matched what we bought from Linda. With all the new bedroom furniture we now had fifteen big drawers and four smaller drawers to fill. I was informed that four of the big drawers had been set aside for my use. All the rest would be needed for Nancy's clothes. As I did not need much space I was okay with the arrangement.

I filled the drawers that had been given to me, and I found that I could comfortably get my underwear, socks, and workout clothes into three drawers and left the fourth empty. Upon noticing this, Nancy asked, "Are you not using that drawer?" She then approached with several articles of clothing in her hands.

I assured her, "That drawer is my savings drawer. It's for new clothing that I have yet to acquire." I said. She frowned at that. I could tell she really wanted the drawer. She didn't say a word but continued to give me the sad pleading look; first at me, then to the drawer, then back to me. Although it was hers for the taking, I had to say one more thing. "Honey, you can have it if you want it. I just hate to give up my savings drawer when it's already gaining so much interest."

She just shook her head. Of course I knew it might cost me more than it was worth, but I trusted her sense of fairness and the fact that she had the remaining eleven big drawers and the four smaller drawers all to herself. She turned and walked to her own drawers and put away the few items that were in her hands. She never did ask for the savings drawer again, but I did offer it to her several times over the next few months.

After some time had passed Nancy said, "I've decided that I'd rather have less space between us than more. I see you've kept the drawer empty. You've been saving it for me. I want you to keep it even if you never have anything you want to put in it. If we can share each other's space perhaps someday we'll both put something in the savings drawer, and it will help us both grow together."

It takes two to have a relationship. Nancy gave me so many opportunities to learn and grow. I only hoped that I recognized most of them. I used humor to find acceptance to most challenges and even though Nancy was often serious, there was only love in all she presented.

Now getting back to the bookcases, as the year came to an end I was true to my word and never even looked at the TV that was safely packed away in its original box. I was pleased with my patience, and knew I was doing the right thing.

Playoff season for football was fast approaching and the Cowboys had made the playoffs. I am sad to say that at the time this news had little effect on me, so when Nancy came to me one day after work and asked, "Would you like to go shopping with me?" I didn't have a clue what might be in store.

"Sure," I said. "Where are we going?"

"Let's go to ATE," she said.

My curiosity was piqued as we already had the TV and surround sound. She took me into the store and led me to the furniture section where she looked at some entertainment centers. She found one that was inexpensive, yet big enough for the new TV and the surround sound. She looked at me and asked, "This would be easy for you to put together, right?"

"Why yes," I replied. Then we bought it. Within twenty-four hours it was put together, her brother Mike came over to install the surround sound, the Satellite people came out so we had high definition TV–and all this because the Cowboys made the playoffs. It was then I realized how much of a football fan she was. In the space of three days we had a complete home entertainment system. It would be eleven months before the bookcases were built, installed, and painted. It didn't matter. It took many more years for the Cowboys to make the playoffs again.

After the bookcases were completed I was all finished with the house that didn't need anything, because that's why Nancy chose this house. By the way, as you have probably guessed that previous statement was a lie, I still wasn't done. In the years to come we added tile to the kitchen, new floors throughout, new stained bookcases in the office, replaced many of the windows, and painted most of the rooms.

It would be easy for me to believe that the house didn't need anything like Nancy said, and I believe she meant it when she said it. The reality is that those little questions about what we want changes as time goes on. Or as Nancy would put it, "things can always be better." Having an understanding of these things from the beginning allowed us to move past the challenges of moving in together. It allowed us to move somewhat humorously through what would be some of the hardest things to overcome, because they were choices we made together. We came to a place of agreement before we started. Even after we agreed we both knew things might change, and we accepted that possibility.

THE NEXT STEP

I once heard the leading man in a movie say to his leading lady, "When you discover you want to spend the rest of your life with someone, you want the rest of your life to start right away." That's how I felt about Nancy. It would have been wonderful if I had found some special way to ask her to marry me. If I could have found just the right words at just the right place, a special place; something that would make it so unforgettable and special that it would have been the grandest proposal ever. That didn't happen. What happened was no matter how hard I tried I just couldn't think of anything that was worthy of her.

If you have ever heard the saying, "Money burning a hole in your pocket," you will understand how I felt having that engagement ring in my pocket for so long. Finally, one night I could wait no longer. She was sitting on the couch and I just walked over knelt down on one knee and asked her to marry me. At first she just looked at me. After what seemed like twenty minutes she said "Yes." I put the ring on her finger and looked into her eyes. "It took you a while to answer," I said. "Are you sure?"

"Yes," she said. "I just wasn't expecting you to ask so soon." Even I was surprised at the words that came out of my mouth there in our living room. The most unusual thing about the proposal was how ordinary it was, but when I looked up at her, her smile said the same thing as her lips had said earlier, "Yes, I will marry you."

I think every life has moments like that; times when we wish we could have done more or been more grand or even just kept our mouth shut. Nancy and I called these moments, "Things that we'll laugh about at Thanksgiving." Sometimes these things were embarrassing, and sometimes they didn't seem funny at all at the time, but time is the thing that separates us from our judgment of the moment. Time gives us the opportunity to gain insight, and understanding, and let's face it; we all need something to talk about on Thanksgiving.

THE WEDDING BANDS

Nancy decided that the next logical step would be to pick out our wedding bands. The ring that Nancy wanted was a simple one; a solitaire diamond inset into a white gold wedding band, so that it would not catch on fabric. She understood that being inset the diamond would not be quite as brilliant as it would not catch as much light.

I would buy two rings for myself; one for when we went out or were entertaining, and a second titanium ring that I would wear while at work as a home improvement contractor. We had a budget for all three rings. The budget for both of my rings was smaller than the budget for hers. I had no problem with this.

Many may think that buying a piece of jewelry should bring joy, but to Nancy, it could actually be the most inhumane type of torture ever invented. This could be true for me also, if I had not had an understanding of Nancy. Shopping with Nancy involved her seeing as many options as possible before making a decision. This often involved going to many different stores within a mall or shopping village. Put yourself in Nancy's shoes, and imagine, if you can, that you are going to purchase a ring that you will probably wear for the rest of your life. It must go with everything you own. It should be impressive but not overpowering, and once on it must feel comfortable and secure. Also, you have to like it. All of these things had to be considered, and more: This was one decision that she would have to live with the rest of her life. That's how stressful this event was.

I will say that the entire process took several weeks. We went to a total of twelve different jewelry stores. This may not seem like much, until you consider spending about an hour in each one. The more rings we looked at the more they all looked alike. No single ring set itself apart from what we considered to be ordinary. It seemed like there was only one ring, and it was passed from store to store, where each salesperson tried to tell us it was unique and different. This didn't fool Nancy. She knew exactly what she wanted and no one had shown it to her, yet.

At one point I thought about getting one custom made to the picture she had in her head. I suggested this to her as we were in yet another store with the kind saleslady standing behind the counter placing the many rings back into the display. She gave me a sort of blank look. It was then I realized she had no real idea what the ring she wanted looked like. The saleslady picked up on this immediately.

"Nancy," she said. "Why don't you just try on whatever catches your eye? Perhaps what you want will come into clearer focus if you move in a different direction."

Nancy looked in the case and gazed at a ring with three diamonds set in white gold well above the band. It looked harmless in the display, but when she placed it on her finger the ring sucked all the light from the room and held it for a second, and then released it blindingly like a beacon that promised only prosperity, happiness, and joy for the rest of our lives. The ring spoke to her, telling her of how much they belonged together and how with it she would never again live in darkness. With this ring she would become the envy of everyone she knew, and live a rich full life. Nancy then spoke words I never expected to hear from the mouth of an engineer, "It's so sparkly."

Nancy never even tried to take it off. She just stared at it like a mother looks at her newborn child. They both knew they were meant to be together. It was even the right size. As a matter of fact the only thing that didn't fit was the price. It was more than twice the budget.

I handed the clerk my credit card and she gave the box to Nancy who slowly took the ring off her finger, and placed it in the box. She never took her eyes off the box even while taking my arm as we walked out to the car in silence. As I reached to open the car door Nancy all at once stood up straight and looked at me as if she had just spent our fortune on some magic beans.

"The ring costs more than twice as much as you were supposed to spend," she said in a startled voice. "Didn't you hear the voices in your head?"

As I looked at her I realized how much I loved her, and how I would never ever, as long as we lived, say no to her. "Honey, I didn't hear the voices in my head. I couldn't hear anything over the voices in your head." She never said another word about how much the ring cost.

I realized at that moment that whatever she said she wanted, the one she would ultimately choose would actually be at least twice as big, twice as grand, and at least twice the price. The voice I needed to listen to was the one in her heart, not her head, and the answer would always be yes.

Chapter 6

Sunday May 6, 2012, 7:17 a.m.

When I stepped out of the room I was given a chair to sit in right outside the door. I immediately began to pray. It started with a prayer for you to have peace, no matter how that looked. Next I prayed for me; I prayed for forgiveness for my cowardice. I prayed for forgiveness; that God would forgive me for my selfishness when it came to you, I couldn't imagine a life without you. I prayed that if these were your last moments on earth that I had not made them an agony for you. I prayed that I made the right decision, and if I had, that you would be able to tell me.

THE WEDDING–2008

Once the decision was made to get married it was time to start planning the wedding. I had figured that since we had both been through this before it would be relatively easy.

Some of my friends insisted that a wedding was just a big party. How hard can it be to plan a party? You get some chips, some drinks, put on some music and decide where you're going to have it. No problem. My friends were wrong. A wedding is not a big party. It is the leading cause of divorce. It is the most difficult challenge a couple can face followed closely by moving.

It defines priorities for both the husband and the wife, and when these priorities do not fall into alignment this simple gathering has the potential to turn into the gateway to hell itself.

When it comes to weddings, being foolish comes easy to a man. We assume things and then deny the complexity of what we believe to be true. We believe that others should know and understand how simple things are, and being simple-minded, things seem simple to us. This is not so. I believe a wedding takes at least four hundred thousand people to plan and execute. All of these people must work in perfect harmony, doing exactly what the bride says as soon as she says it. Then they must do it again, right this time, as quickly as possible.

The alternative is to hire a wedding planner. If you hire a wedding planner, it will take about ten people working in perfect harmony and the cost will be higher than you ever expected. The price does not include the dress, the cake, the church, the tuxedos, the food, the drink, the band, the DJ, the transportation, the hotels, or the cost of the wedding planner. Knowing these things ahead of time will not make anything go smoother.

The first thing we needed to do was to set a date. It needed to be soon enough that we had something to look forward to, and far enough away so we had time to plan the wedding. We also had to consider holidays, birthdays, and where we would honeymoon. No one wants to go to the beach in February unless you're headed to Australia. We started with choosing where we would like to go on our honeymoon. We both wrote on a piece of paper where we would like to go. I wrote St. Augustine, FL. We then folded the papers and handed them to each other so we could each see what the other had written. She wrote St. Augustine, FL. Now we had to choose whose paper would be where we would go. Some things can be simple after all.

We then decided that May would be a good month to be there. Warm, but not the full heat of the summer. We picked the seventeenth of May because it was a Saturday. After all, people work on weekdays and Sundays are for church. I remembered the challenges that we faced with the ring so when things went surprisingly smooth for us, I started to pay attention. Lists were made, and tasks were assigned, and we began what would be the best time of our life up to that point. This was not what I expected.

It amazed most of those we knew how easy life was for us on so many levels, yet the one thing that seemed inescapable, was the constant reminder of cancer. I wondered if we were without this condition, would we be aware of all the wonder and fullness of life that we were experiencing.I knew it was worth thinking about but let's face it; we had a wedding to plan.

THE INVITATIONS

Who can I invite? Both of us came from large families. If I had invited all my relatives and their children there would not have been enough airplanes to get them here. If Nancy had invited all of her relatives the highways would have been jammed for weeks. As for our friends, well they lived close enough to walk. We decided to have the wedding at our church so we were limited to about 80 people. This worked out well because now we had an excuse as to how many would get an invitation.

I knew that since my family lived in the Northeast, few if any would be able to attend. I also knew that Nancy's family, living several hours away, would all be able to attend. What I did not know is that they would all *want* to attend. Nancy suggested we set up a priority system to efficiently determine how to select who to invite.

This was a very comprehensive system of checks and balances that included such things as income, (for the gifts), embarrassment factor, (for entertainment), plays well with others factor, (keep the brawling to a minimum), the can't be bothered but always sends nice gifts group, and most importantly the likelihood that they would not attend factor, (we could invite my whole family because they won't be able to get here).

It seemed like a foolproof system. As a matter of fact we only had one glitch. My brother Norm, and his wife Barb, decided to travel from New Hampshire to Texas for our big day. Apparently we forgot to add the, "I can't believe they're coming all the way from New Hampshire group." Luckily Norm and Barb, like all my family could easily fit in, in Texas.

Note to self, remind them not to wear cowboy hats.....

I was charged with filling out the invitations and getting them mailed. I have this awful reputation of having good penmanship and besides, no one else would do it. I agreed because it kept me busy working on the wedding, and it was something that I could get wedding points for. Working on the wedding is not the same as getting wedding points. Everyone works on the wedding (not necessarily point worthy), but only those who are given a task that no one else wants to do will get wedding points.

Over the course of the wedding preparations, I figure I managed to rack up 792 wedding points, out of a maximum 1,000. I got those making phone calls and securing musicians and doing all the things that a wedding planner would do. The difference was that I got the points instead of the money, and any husband will tell you that the points are way more important than the money.

The 208 points that I missed went to Elisabeth, who picked up the wedding cake and transported it forty miles from the bakery to the church. I think Elizabeth left the day before because she was afraid to drive faster than two miles per hour as long as it was in her SUV. If necessary I would have given her some of my wedding points, as this was the one thing that is always the most important non-human part of any wedding.

THE DRESS

Nancy told me she wanted an off-white dress that was nice but not a traditional wedding gown. She wanted something simple yet elegant. We started our search in some of the better department stores where she normally shopped.

Sadly, like the ring, nothing could be found that was what she wanted. I was beginning to see a pattern, but when it came to the dress she assured me that she would not compromise, on what was in her mind, appropriate. After hitting all the high-end department stores over the next several weeks with no luck, we found ourselves in a shopping mall that we normally would not go to. This mall had some different stores and even some that catered to weddings.

One bridal shop had many nontraditional dresses that were appropriate for second and even third weddings. She found several that she liked and asked my preference. I responded honestly stating the ones that I liked and in the order of my preference, assuring her that it was her choice and I would be happy with whatever her decision was. She asked me to leave and return in about thirty minutes so she could try them on without me seeing her. I understood it is supposed to be "bad luck" for the bride to be seen by her future husband in her dress before the wedding, so off I went. I returned in forty-five minutes so she would have plenty of time to try on the dresses that she had yet to find.

When I returned the bridal shop was packed. Everyone in the shop was excitedly standing around her as they boxed up the beautiful white full-length wedding gown that she finally chose. They congratulated her and shook my hand and told me how lucky I was. It was then I was told by the other shoppers that Nancy had to get, "that traditional wedding dress in white" that was nothing like she described because when she walked out of the dressing room with it on even the people outside the shop ran in to look at her.

They told me she had gotten at least four other proposals on the spot from men who were better looking, younger, in better shape, and made more money. They told me I was the luckiest man on the planet and had better treat her right or else. So I put on my sternest look and politely said, "Okay."

In the past, Nancy had settled for less than what she truly wanted. When she would find her way to her true desire however, now she would not hesitate to embrace it. She only needed someone to let her know that the world was hers if she wanted it. She wanted to live the dream, and it didn't matter if it wasn't perfect the first time she married. She was willing to try it again, and in doing so it would be the first real marriage for her. It made her choice of dresses not only appropriate, but desirable.

On the way to the car I let her know how pleased I was with her choice. I was glad she had a traditional white dress that was all she wanted. I asked myself what this meant about our future. It said she saw there was something very special about us. I thought about the men she dated over the years; professional, successful, handsome, and yet she left them behind and chose me. It was the highest compliment I could have received. Now it was up to me to live up to her dream.

As we entered the car she let me know it was a little more than she wanted to spend. How could it matter? She was priceless.

I wonder sometimes, what would we do if we didn't need permission? If you're a grownup you might say, "I don't need permission." Yet many of us, including myself, let societal norms dictate almost everything we do. Perhaps this is why the world admires the original, and no statue has ever been raised to a critic.

Chapter 7

Sunday May 6, 2012, 8:00 a.m.

It was a lonely time right outside the room. I began to make phone calls; first to your brother Mike who would call the rest of our family. I made calls to our minister and to those friends closest to you. I told them all that I wasn't sure if you would make it.

A while later Dr. Weston came out and said, "We got her back Mr. Carrier. We had to do blood transfusions because her oxygen levels were so low. Nancy's blood was very acidic, and at that level did not support life. We needed to do an emergency tracheotomy to keep her ventilated. Because of the restriction in her throat, this was very difficult and some air escaped under her skin. As a result, her face and neck look extremely swollen. The puffiness will go away in a few days. We did a lot of work to get her back. She's a very sick girl. I must caution you not to expect too much."

I stopped listening after, "we got her back." You, my beloved, were alive.

THE WEDDING DAY–2008

On the day of the wedding I was at a hotel that was about fifteen miles from the church. My best man George had set this up so I had no transportation other than him and I was as nervous as I have ever been. George would drive me to the hotel where we would be spending our wedding night, and I would drop off the luggage, then we'd head to the church where I would change into my tuxedo. Not too bad.

All the preparation in the world does nothing to calm the nerves of the bride and groom the morning of the wedding. The phrase from Dickens, "It was the best of times, it was the worst of times," could as easily have been written about the day of someone's wedding as it was about the French Revolution. This is the day where it all comes together. It is the Super Bowl of a person's life, and like the Super Bowl, you can never plan for everything.

When we got to the hotel we found that we couldn't leave the luggage there until 3:00 p.m. The wedding started at 2:30. Anyone could see the problem here. I explained our predicament to the all-powerful desk clerk who proclaimed that there was nothing he could do. There was no way to change the policy because it was written in **bold type** and could not be erased or altered, and not only that, it was *laminated,* which meant that it was at least a federal crime to in anyway deviate from the process.

It took several minutes of negotiations that involved lots of weeping and whining (mostly on his part) before we came to an agreement to be allowed to leave the five bags behind the desk and he would have someone take them up to our room later in the day before 6:00 p.m. when we were scheduled to arrive.

As it turned out the only thing that would have made it completely and totally impossible would have been for the laminated rule sheet to be in a locked glass case behind the counter. As everyone knows when the sheet is laminated in bold print on company letterhead in a locked glass case behind the counter the rule is enforced by penalty of death, or at least being yelled at for a long time in front of your mother and father. No one wants that kind of stress.

This turned out to be my biggest obstacle for the day. I figured I got off easy.

Nancy's day of preparation would start at our home with the prep team coming over to help her get ready. The prep team consisted of: Sherry, the Maid of Honor; Amy, the hairdresser;

and Lauren, the makeup artist. Janis, our coordinator, was at the Celebration of Life Church taking care of last-minute details, and finishing up everything that still needed attention.

Having these ladies in place was invaluable as they tended to all the details that would otherwise panic Nancy. Nancy was able to trust and surrender the tasks to them, and on this most important of days, they would not disappoint us. The decorations were perfect; the food was on time and fresh, the wedding and groom's cakes had been delivered intact, the music was prepared, and everyone was right where they needed to be. Well, almost everyone.

Back at the house, completely out of the range of my radar, an incident was unfolding that would shake Nancy to her very foundation. The dream team had arrived at the house on time. As our hairdresser was entering the house with her arms full of all manner of hair products that could rival Jack's magic beans with their power of transformation, she was unable to close the front door behind her. It remained open for a few moments before it was noticed.

After they realized it was open, a cat count was conducted. We only had two cats, Luke and Chewy. They were named after characters from a popular movie (*Star Wars,* if you haven't already guessed) because they wouldn't answer to any of the classic literature names we tried. After a quick and desperate search they could only find Chewy. This was a big problem.

The dream team and Nancy started the more extensive search by checking the rooms of the house to see if Luke had been locked up by accident. When this happened he would always be waiting at the door poised for a quick escape, but after the last door had been opened we were still missing one cat. The ladies then began an outside search going under shrubs, climbing trees, going house to house, even checking storm drains, all with no luck.

The clock seemed to tick faster and faster picking up speed as they searched. The clock moved like an eighteen-wheeler traveling down a mountain pass with no breaks, heading toward a hairpin turn that would cause it to plummet off the edge of a cliff and land crashing and catching fire on the church where our wedding was to take place. The only good part would be that no one would be there because we'd be searching for the damn cat.

After searching for what felt like several hours, or fifteen minutes if you insist on accuracy, our feline friend was found in our bedroom hiding under the bed. Somehow no one thought to check there. The world was once again spinning in greased grooves.

Even with the setback, Nancy and her helpers arrived at the church in plenty of time, and both Nancy and I knew in our hearts that we were going to have plenty to talk about on Thanksgiving.

THE CEREMONY

We had some of the pictures taken for my side of the family and me before the wedding to save time. This also gave me something to do so I stayed out of trouble. I have been a guest at lots of weddings and I know how the wait for it to start can drag out, so we tried to keep everything moving smoothly so there was always something going on to keep everyone's attention. This also made the time fly for me.

No sooner did we finish the pictures, the music was playing letting us know it was time for me to get to the front of the church. I glanced into the sanctuary and found it packed. We had a capacity for about eighty and every seat was filled. I thought to myself, *standing room only*. Then took the first steps that would take me to the front. As soon as I arrived I turned to look, anxiously searching for a glimpse of Nancy.

All at once this absolute vision of beauty and elegance stepped into the doorway. The sight of her literally took the breath from my body. In that moment I completely understood what the people at the store where she bought the dress were talking about. I really was blessed to have her as my bride.

Her father had her arm and walked her to the front to stand next to me. The way he looked at her I could tell how in awe he was at the beauty that was at his side. She meant the world to him as well. Had I been in his shoes I do not think it would be easy to give her away. Still he stepped aside. Nancy looked at me and smiled and everything in the world came to a standstill. There was only Nancy and I in the whole universe, and we were enough.

Our vows were exchanged in what seemed like seconds, although the minister had us up there for close to twenty minutes. There were candles to light, rings to exchange, and roses to be given to one another. I can honestly say that I enjoyed this ceremony that represented our commitment to each other. It helped to show our friends and family the depth of our relationship in an outward manner, but this outward ceremony could not compare to the depth our personal relationship had already achieved.

Perhaps this is true of most couples. We spend months setting the groundwork, building the foundation for a relationship that will weather any storm. After it's done we have an open house party to celebrate, but the work is not finished, and ideally the improvements and additions will go on throughout our lives. The party is just to show others the accomplishment and commitment we have to the project, and to celebrate this first milestone of a larger, much larger project; a shared lifetime with someone deeply loved.

We felt supported by each other, our families, and friends. It was elegant, magical, regal, and most important it was a dream come true for us both. It's an amazing experience to get married, but I would be remiss if I did not at least mention one of the grandest reasons for getting married in the first place, going on the honeymoon.

It would seem the more important something is, the greater the tragedy in anything going wrong. I know in sports, one small mistake can cost you the game or even the season. Yet we somehow lose sight of the fact that so much went into the event. During the course of any event there can be more wins than losses. Until writing this book if anyone asked me about our wedding the only things that would have slipped my mind would have been getting the bags to the room and losing the cat.

On the flip side, it is these challenges that also add to the worth of such accomplishment. In the end I choose to put the things that made this time so very special at the front of my memory. The challenges may be stored in my mind, but the sheer majesty of that day will forever be in my heart, right where it belongs.

Chapter 8

Sunday May 6, 2012, 8:34 a.m.

They said you would be taken to ICU in a few minutes. Your brother Mike and Rev. Lari came by while I was waiting, and I let them know what happened and how your heart had stopped but I didn't know for how long. I told them the doctor said things didn't look good. Mike and I cried together. Rev. Lari and I prayed and we all waited.

GOING HOME–2008

The wedding was a success, the honeymoon was over (sorry no honeymoon details here). We had been together for over a year and I knew Nancy better than I had known any other person in my life. The focus we had placed on honesty had brought our relationship to a new depth of understanding that amazed me, and we had just begun. I had always thought that after the initial joy and excitement at the beginning of a relationship the work begins. For many the work of a new marriage means having children; but for the both of us, who had more life experience than younger newlyweds, it would be about balancing living with dying.

I say balancing but really it's about living without the constant thought of dying a slow and painful death. That's a harsh statement. But it's the truth. For most of us this thought will not dominate our consciousness until we are of advancing years, or we have been given some very disturbing news from a doctor. It could be a lot of work to keep the thought of impending doom from dominating our lives. There could also be the added concern of having the condition devastate us financially. The honeymoon was over; it was time to face the fact that we would not be living what others would consider a normal life, but in the middle of the word life is "if," and although we control the direction our lives take, physical death is always the end of the journey.

Nancy had chosen the holistic road of treatment because there was little choice in her mind about what could be done, but holistic, means more than just praying and eating good food; it means whole. This form of treatment involves changing one's lifestyle by choice. It's not necessarily the choice of a competent authority like the medical doctor. In fact in some cases it's against the advice of the medical profession. Psychologically and metaphysically this can cause problems. We must ask ourselves, "Do I really believe that I know more about my body than this person who spent eight-plus years studying how the human body works? Well, DO YOU? Are you willing to bet your life on it?"

Actually, it would be more accurate to say, "Are you willing to bet the years you have left?"

We all have to live, or possibly die, with the choices we make for ourselves. Nancy made her treatment choice before we were dating. At this point in our relationship I could see no reason to challenge her decision. I had experienced how Nancy made decisions. There was no reason to believe that her decision was not in her best interest. I admired her for that. I chose to take this path with her knowing the barrier that might lie ahead of us.

My belief is that no problem can be solved consistently without all pertinent information being given. The doctor knows, to a large extent, how the body operates, at least in a mechanical sense. The patient knows, for the most part, how it has been treated for the time preceding the condition. The word diagnosis is derived from two Latin words; di, meaning two and gnosis meaning knowledge. In other words, two people who know half of the information that could be used to create a solution. Both of you know something, but neither knows everything. This is not stated to demean or diminish the medical profession.

We, as a society, place a lot of pressure on medical doctors to know everything about us and heal us when we abuse our bodies. We often blame them when we refuse to change our diet or lifestyle, because they can't give us a pill that will make the condition that we ourselves have created, go away.

When Nancy chose the holistic route for her treatment, it wasn't because the doctor was incompetent; it was because when she looked at her situation honestly, she knew that she had a better chance of changing her condition than he did. This did not mean he was out of the picture. He was very much involved and as much as we let him he participated in our treatment. We considered him a blessing and honored his participation even when it was just as an advisor.

I have seen so many others in my lifetime go along with whatever the doctor said, even when that meant gaining only a few months of life that would be spent in agony from the side effects of the treatment. In one case in my family it meant over a month of severe pain, where the patient was not even able to communicate with us. I found it very easy to support Nancy, but we both did our research before we acted. It was, in my opinion, the only decision she could make. It was about choosing to live more fully, even if it cost her a shorter life.

As for me, I chose to be part of her treatment team. This meant that I would eat as she ate, drink as she drank, and live a clean, healthy lifestyle. My desire was to be intimate with Nancy; to know her journey. I could not duplicate her cancer in me, but I could share her restrictions. Nancy told me, by doing this, she felt closer to me. Actions like this helped us connect at a much deeper level to each other.

I already had a good idea of her treatment plan. Her diet was mostly organic, raw foods, to boost her immune system. If supplements were required, they had to be made of real food, as opposed to chemicals. To treat the mental aspect she would keep positive by reinforcing her awareness of any positive changes in her condition and read and study others who had eliminated cancer in their lives through meditation/prayer/faith/belief, exercise, diet, or using it all.

We also used chiropractic, acupuncture, and other healing modalities, that were usually reserved for those who had little or no hope. These things were not covered by insurance. It would be up to us to pay our way, but that's just the way we wanted it.

The routine was very easy to adjust to. I would get up before my alarm, and then I would hear Nancy's alarm go off. She would push the snooze button and then go back to lying down. This would happen at least three times. We would then prepare a smoothie for breakfast and shower and be off. I would leave around 6:30 but Nancy didn't have to leave until about 7:30 to be at work by 8:00. I was always out before her, and made sure that she was all set before I left.

This worked well, as we had some space between needing to shower and use the bathroom. We could have breakfast together and then be out of each other's way to prepare for our day. We both had plenty of time to get ready.

Nancy had worked at a company that made airplane wings for the last twenty-nine years. In the last twenty-eight years she had not been to work on time. She was always between eight and fifteen minutes late. Even if she got up earlier, she always seemed to find something that would cause her some delay. It amazed me how consistent she was. It was obvious that she was good enough at her job for this minor factor to be of any concern.

There were many mornings where, per her instructions I got her up earlier so she would have enough time to get to work before eight. This usually involved me physically connecting with her in a non-combative way to help her get moving. The theory was that she had a routine. If we got her up fifteen minutes earlier, then, theoretically this strategy would prove successful. This was not the case in real life.

Whether we are habitually early, or habitually late, the problem is never the clock. It would, however, be erroneous on my part to say I knew what could be done to solve the issue of her consistent tardiness, but I did have an understanding that what we were doing would not prove to be successful on a consistent basis. As a matter of fact, it had a success rate of zero. We went so far as getting up thirty minutes early and Nancy got to work that day later than she had in years. That particular day she was over twenty minutes late to work.

As a society, we seem to have a propensity to treat the symptoms rather than the disease. This can give short-term relief but does nothing to solve the problem or change the issue. If Nancy and I chose to really solve the problem of her getting to work on time she would have been successful.

The only person that it really mattered to was me; and that was because Nancy said she wanted to solve this issue. I realized after a few days that she really didn't want to change the behaviors that were causing her tardiness. After that we were both just going through the motions. I've heard it said that trying is failing with honor. I hoped this was not the case with the biggest issue in our lives, which had nothing to do with work.

The positive thing about our mornings was that after we got up and made tea we meditated. This was every day; we even started the day like this on our honeymoon. It really made a difference to us that we did this together in the morning. We both believed that our deep connection to our higher power was the one thing that was most important. We wanted to honor the Spirit that we believed had brought us together.

We spent our days like everyone else, with work and then supper. The only thing that broke up the routine was the occasional doctor's appointment. And aside from the minor pain that Nancy experienced when swallowing, it would have been easy to go on like this for many years. We thought that going through this mindless routine each day was living: No big surprises, and the comfort of knowing what was around every corner. It gives us the illusion of control, a sense of non-disturbance if you will.

But the best illusion is still illusion. It was pretending our lives were like other couples who were both healthy. We were living the dream, because that's what it was, a dream. Deep down we knew that sooner or later, it would be time to wake up.

The trick was to not let cancer be the constant focus of our attention. We are all aware that we are ageing. Every year, every month, every week, every day, every minute, and every second, we get older. Not only that, but anyone can die at any time. Yet these things usually do not fill our thoughts. The thought of dying may pop in for a moment every now and then, but it's usually dismissed quickly; at least for the first sixty or so years of our lives. We wanted to be like that.

One thing that helped was getting our affairs in order. I asked Nancy if she knew within a year when she was going to die; she said no. I told her I didn't know either. I told her it could be me who died first. This was something that we conveniently overlooked. After that we made out our wills and set up funeral arrangements. We also took the time to understand each other's wishes. We agreed that whoever was left behind would honor the other's wishes. In this way we were able put some of our fear behind us.

THE LAKE HOUSE

The weekends belonged to us for the most part. Nancy's dad had a house on a lake near Temple, TX. The family called it the cabin, and Nancy wanted me to see it. A lake house, I thought, this could be awesome. We should get out there every chance we get. It was located on a peninsula with two other homes that shared a road/driveway and was separated from the lake road by a gate. The lake road took us to a rural highway. It was a secluded getaway where we could leave the rest of the world behind.

The next weekend we were on our way to the cabin after work. Nancy said, "It's about two hours away and when we get there we'll need to get things unlocked and turn the water on."

This seemed pretty simple, so I nodded okay and sat back in the front seat of her car as we headed to the cabin. Knowing how elegant and refined Nancy was, I could only imagine what the place looked like. She had described it as well above the water on the side of a cliff overlooking Lake Belton. She had gone to a lot of family gatherings there often with more people than came to the Christmas party I had attended. I figured the place must be pretty big.

The traffic was pretty bad that first time out and we had gotten a late start. When we arrived at Seven Coves Road where the cabin was located it was already dark. Seven Coves was a dirt road, and I believe it was cleared by pulling out the bushes and trees, and never filling any of the holes. Our maximum speed was so slow we had to wave a spider to go around us. He was tailgating. Then we were passed by a toad.

I was very surprised that Nancy was willing to take a passenger car down this road. I was thinking this must be what a major earthquake feels like. It felt like it took us twenty minutes to drive the one mile on that dirt road that would take us to the gate.

Nancy pulled out a ring of keys that looked like something a janitor would carry and after a few tries unlocked the gate. We drove in and up a separate driveway, the headlights illuminating a white building. My first thought was, "This can't be it." But it was. With the lights shining on the door, she unlocked a lock on a very rickety screen door. I wondered what good the lock was when you could pull the whole door off piece by piece with your bare hands and very little effort.

Next there was another padlock on the house door along with a dead bolt. I wondered what they had in there that required this much security. By then, Nancy had used four different keys. I later found out that with the things inside that were also locked with the building and the gate combined she would need seven different keys to gain access to the whole cabin. This did not include the shed, which was located in front of the cabin.

After everything was unlocked the water and electric needed to be turned on. Once the inside of the cabin was illuminated it was apparent why they needed so many locks. Obviously, they didn't want anyone to know what the inside of this place looked like. The ceiling fan was at least twenty years old, and the wires were exposed. There were three light fixtures: two hanging fixtures, and one on a second ceiling fan, all three in a seven-foot radius in the kitchen. All of them were at least twenty years old. Bells were going off in my contractor's head.

It was the Frankenstein of houses. It was obviously put together out of spare parts of other houses that had died, and died ugly deaths at that. It had brown recluse spiders, wasps, and termites. The outside paint was peeling and the roof was in need of replacement. The one redeeming quality that it had was that Nancy loved it. That fact made me take a good long look at myself.

After a few days there I began to understand what it was about this place. There were deer in the front yard every morning. The lake was tranquil and quiet with scarcely a motorboat. And with no TV there was none of the usual noise inside the house either. While we were at the cabin the world seemed to stop, our minds quieted, and our hearts rested. I no longer saw the Frankenstein of houses. It was really the featherbed of houses, a place to rest our souls. Now when I looked at myself, I could understand that like the cabin, Nancy saw something in me that gave her the same feeling. So I decided it was time to get to work.

In the next year I repaired the plumbing, replaced the air conditioner, added heat, removed the old leaky wood stove, put in a water purification system, replaced the front door and the storm door, and had the locks changed so that you could access everything with only three keys. In all the weekends I worked on it I never felt tired. I always went home rested. It was amazing, but more than that, Nancy was happy.

In our second year of marriage Nancy's dad gave her the keys to the cabin. It belonged to her now. He said he didn't want to wait till he was gone for her to have it. On our next trip down, we renamed it, "The Lake House." It was our away home, when our home just wasn't enough. We would spend between twelve to twenty weekends a year here at the lake. In all that time, we were never disappointed in being there. It was a place of joy and peace.

I think everyone has something that becomes the main focus of his or her life. I also believe it is our ability to respond to a condition that makes the biggest difference. Everyone seeks some kind of refuge from striving each day. Our refuge became the lake house. Somehow, cancer could not find us here.

We simplified the lake house by removing the things that were not needed. I began the repairs, and completed most of them. Though some may look at what needed to be done as just more work, a burden becomes a blessing with the right perspective; and work becomes pleasure. Like our relationship, we never tired of working on it. Once all the distractions were removed the true beauty was revealed and we found comfort each time we allowed its beauty to gently envelop our beings.

Chapter 9

Sunday May 6, 2012, 9:09 a.m.

When your room was prepared, we walked to the ICU waiting area. I was the only one allowed in at first but I let everyone know I would keep them informed. I went through the glass doors to see you lying in your hospital bed with more wires and tubes coming out of you than our surround sound receiver. Your face was as Dr. Weston had said, very puffy on the right side with the puffiness extending down to your throat. This was air that had gotten under your skin while they were trying to get the breathing tube inserted. The breathing tube was connected to a suctioning contraption, which was connected to a respirator.

I could see monitors for blood oxygen level, blood pressure, respiration, heart rate, and even some that I didn't recognize. I knew all these machines were helping you, but I also knew the one reason you were still here. I believed you stayed alive because you wanted to. I felt there was a very good chance that I made the right decision. All I needed now was for you to tell me.

EXTREME HEALTH–2008

Extreme Health took place in Los Angeles. It was a Friday to Sunday retreat. This event would have presenters at specific time intervals offering us some specific practices, (free) as well as special services or products for discount prices. It was very informative and both Nancy and I took copious notes. As with most events of this kind there were a few presenters that made a big impression on us.

For Nancy, it was a musician whose music could take a person into a healing state of consciousness, and a doctor who could tell you what was wrong with you and what you needed by reading your pulse. We bought some CDs from the musician, and signed up for a reading with the doctor.

At the appointment with the doctor, knowing nothing about Nancy or her condition, he told her she had a growth in her neck under her jaw. He then suggested an herbal treatment that she could purchase from the nurses on the way out, as well as some dietary suggestions. She purchased the treatment and we began using it right away, while listening to the music each morning during meditation.

My belief, when it comes to most things, is that what we believe plays a big part in what is created in our lives. In other words, if one really believes that eating hotdogs and ice cream will make you thin, then it will. Nancy believed in the power of healing through music, she believed that this doctor using the pulse method would help her healing. I also remembered how I was given this retreat. I felt guided that I was brought here after not signing up when it would have cost me money to attend. There was a reason I was brought in but I hadn't yet put my finger on it.

I found great interest in the health effects of rebounding. The rebounder promoted healing by fully engaging the lymph system. The human body has no lymph pump and the action of using this rebounder circulated the hormones and healing chemicals throughout the body. It also improves balance and promotes a healthy weight; both things that were desirable for Nancy and me.

The other thing that caught my interest was something called, "The Journey." The Journey was a process by which one would explore one's consciousness to discover memories that might be contributing to a health condition, or an undesirable chronic behavior that one might be experiencing. When a memory was discovered it was brought to light, re-evaluated, and released through forgiveness.

The first day there Nancy noticed I was walking with a slight limp. After she mentioned it I began to notice it too, although I could find nothing that would cause me to walk that way. Since all of us got to have an experience of the Journey process I decided to use this as my experiment.

Our Journey experience began with our presenter taking us through a guided introspection to find our issue and see if we could come to a place of forgiveness. This took about twenty minutes. It worked wonders for me. When I finished I knew my limp was gone.

I was quite impressed with the process and told Nancy that I would very much like to go to the next Journey event in Sedona, Arizona. I felt sure this was our best choice of treatment for her as well, even though she was not interested in going. I felt if I went I could learn the process and bring it back to teach Nancy what I learned, we could use it to help each other. Nancy agreed and I signed up for the Journey intensive and advanced skills. That marked the end of Extreme Health. We both felt we were moving in a direction that would add years to our life together.

More than anything else, we focused on improving the quality of life for Nancy, and thereby, for myself. I knew it was not in my ability to cure her or anyone else, but I wanted to make sure I learned all I could to keep her on the right path spiritually, mentally, and physically. It was at times like these that we realized how fully committed to each other we really were.

The next morning we decided to take a look around the area before going to the airport. We decided to take this opportunity to see the Pacific Ocean, and even though it was a bit chilly, we decided to dip our toes in. As we walked along the beach listening to the waves, we talked of our experiences at the seminar.

"I feel good about the doctor," she told me. "He seems so kind and gentle."

"Go with your heart Honey, trust your intuition," I said.

"I wish I was better at that. I know you trust yours and it's always worked for you. But since I got news of the cancer I haven't trusted my body very much. Actually, I feel very betrayed by it."

"I can understand that. I wish I could give some sage advice on what happened to you, but frankly I'm just as baffled as you are. I'm not sure what it would be like for me to change my diet to eating healthy and a year later find out I had cancer. I might feel the same as you."

"David, what happened to you during the Journey?"

"When we got to the part where I went through the body looking for a memory, I went to the leg that had the limp and found a memory of being born. That leg was holding me up and the priest was blessing me or something, and all of a sudden I was slapped. I felt like I wasn't supposed to be here. I wanted him to let go but I felt like if he did, I'd be hurt more. Through the process I discovered that it was okay that he held me and I didn't need to be held anymore. I could support myself."

"Did you know your limp is gone?"

"Yes, I know. I felt a lot different afterward too. I still trust my body and I feel like this will be a way for me to be able to feel more. That's why I wanted to sign up."

"I was glad you did. Maybe you can help me and teach me after you get back from Sedona."

"You know I will."

She looked at the sand for a long time as we walked along the beach before looking up at me and smiling. "I'm glad we have each other Honey Bunny."

"Me too," I said.

We walked a while longer before getting to our car and then heading off to catch a flight home. Nancy was now armed with her new natural medicine and I was now armed with several books to read before I got to plan a trip to Sedona. There was much to learn for us both.

We both spent much of our lives in schools; with both formal education and esoteric teachings. Nancy had certifications in many modalities, including hypnosis, coaching, Spiritual Practitioner, SCUBA open water diving, and a BS degree in biology. She was always learning something new. I was the same way, with Kenpo karate, Family Teaching, Behavioral Management, kids coaching, grief support, bartending, farming, and even ballroom dancing. But this time it was different. We were both looking for answers that would take us beyond what the medical profession had been studying for decades, with greater minds than ours. Still, we had one thing going for us. All things being equal, the rabbit will win the race with the fox. The fox is running for his dinner, the rabbit is running for its life.

Chapter 10

Sunday May 6, 2012, 11:13 a.m.

A new doctor, Dr. Edelman, came in and said, "Nancy has been through a lot. She has had trouble breathing for some time. In her weakened condition the hardest thing for her to do is breathe on her own. She is currently being sedated so that the ventilator can breathe for her. If she were to wake, breathing on a different rhythm than the machine could cause damage to her lungs. I want to keep her sedated for three days to heal, and strengthen her body then wake her up and examine her before putting her back under for the surgeon to install the permanent breathing tube. Do you have any questions Mr. Carrier?"

I told him, "Not right now. I think we just want to go forward and see where we are. I'm sure when Nancy wakes up she'll have plenty of questions for you."

Dr. Edelman got a very concerned look on his face, and said, "I'm not sure you know just how serious your wife's condition is Mr. Carrier. I don't think you should get your hopes too high."

At that point we both looked at you. I said, "Doc, she's not in a coma right?" He shook his head no. "She's not dead right?" He shook his head no. "Well she must be alive then." He just looked at me. "Let's be grateful for what we've got and go from there, okay."

THE JOURNEY–2008

The Journey intensive and advanced skills workshop took place in Sedona, Arizona. This is a town known for holistic healing and energy vortexes. I knew Nancy had been there and I was surprised that she had chosen to stay home. I would miss her, but I knew someone in the small town of Jerome, which was just a short drive from Sedona.

I could save on a few nights in a hotel, as well as visit an old friend. His name was Randy, and he believed in healing the body with nutrition and divine belief. He was a gentle soul with an aura of peace about him. The kind of person you meet for the first time, and you feel you've known each other for years. I was looking forward to seeing him as much as going to the Journey, maybe more.

As the time approached to leave I noticed a feeling of apprehension rising in my gut. I had become familiar with the process through the books I had been asked to read and what I had experienced at Extreme Health, but this just seemed to add to the unease that I was already experiencing.

The woman who is credited for creating the Journey is Brandon Bays. She herself had cancer in her abdomen and was able to heal herself through the process she discovered. Since her discovery she has helped thousands of others including myself heal from both chronic and even terminal illnesses.

I was about to enter an event where I would sit with a total stranger and undergo a process where I would be required to speak out loud about memories I had done my best to bury for the last forty years. And I was paying for it. It all sounded ridiculous until I thought about how Brandon used this to cure her cancer. I knew I couldn't do this process for Nancy. It had to be for me, but if it worked for me then I would know it could work for Nancy. I would know because I had done it. When I thought about it this way it was easier to go, but the apprehension was still there. I figured once I got to Randy's house I'd be okay. It was not the case. Although he was an excellent host and gave me an amazing place to sleep, I was up most of the night.

I left for Sedona and found a hotel close to the spiritual center where the event was being held. Even though I knew what to expect at a seminar, I didn't know what to expect from myself, emotionally. I found out quickly as I entered the building. I was feeling every emotion I ever had all at once.

Our presenter was Skip, the same man who took us through the process at Extreme Health. That did calm me down a bit. He led us through the different stages of the Journey Process, explaining each one. Then he took a volunteer from the team of volunteer trainers, and practitioners who were there. I'll call him John. John was given a full Journey Process facilitated by Skip right there on the stage in front of us all.

First John identified the emotion that was strongest for him. Then he went into that emotion to see what was beneath it. Skip would then ask if any memory showed up at that level. If the answer was no he would continue to ask until a memory was revealed. Once a memory had been uncovered, Skip would stop asking. He continued to "drop through" these emotions until the emotions changed from being contractive to expansive: Contractive being emotions that shut us down like: hate, anger, and fear; expansive being emotions that empower us like: love, joy, and bliss.

Once the expansive emotions were reached he dropped through two more emotional levels and then moved back up, washing through each level until the level of the memory was reached. At this level an intensive forgiveness process was facilitated. After forgiveness was achieved, John was led to washing up through the remaining layers, and finishing with a letter that solidifies the learning that has taken place.

John was very open to the process and his commitment let us see by his example just what could be uncovered by the Journey. We all thanked him, and then Skip asked us to take a break then find a partner to begin our own process. We would pair off and one of us would give a process to the other, then when we were finished we would switch.

I found a partner, and introduced myself. I asked her if she would be willing to swap processes and she said yes. Her name was Anne. I would receive first. I completed the first part of the process easily dropping through the layers, and finding a memory. I expanded and I forgave, and washed up easily. The whole thing took about forty minutes, and when I was done I felt amazing. My partner, Anne, had some difficulty, and I, being inexperienced, was of no help, but with the help from the practitioners and trainers, my partner completed in about fifty minutes.

I was very excited and enthusiastic about coming back the next two days. The second day was for a slightly different Journey Process, and the third day was to learn advanced skills that could enhance our Journey experience. It was on advanced skills day that something happened that changed how I looked at forgiveness forever.

Several years earlier I had injured my sixth cervical vertebrae: CV6. It caused me debilitating pain for the first two weeks and during that time I saw my chiropractor every day. After that, it went to three times a week for several months, then twice a week for several more months, then once a week for the remainder of the year. After that, the pain was manageable and only got bad when I had to drive for more than an hour, or if I had to sit in a chair for more than about thirty minutes. It hurt but I could manage it. The only thing that worried me about the injury was that it might get worse as I got older. I had been told that in the future I might require surgery to relieve the pain. I hadn't given it much thought until the third day of the Journey intensive.

Advanced skills day was as exciting as the other days but with all of us having several Journeys under our belt we felt better about going into the next process. All I will say about what I learned is that it was incredibly insightful and remarkably entertaining. At the end of the day I was ready for my Journey. I found my partner; I'll call her Alice. Alice was in a wheelchair. She told me she tried to attend the Journey weekend several other times, each time injuring her same leg days before the start. This last time she broke her leg. Actually, she said she shattered the bone.

"I figured if I didn't go now, even with the broken leg, I'd be in fear the rest of my life. The up side was I got special treatment at the airport, and the hotel, and I'm pretty sure I've gotten past the issue that caused me to do this," she said, pointing to her leg.

"You are a brave girl Alice," I said. "Would you like receive first?"

"Yes," she replied.

Her process went very smoothly and she found forgiveness

easily. Then it was my turn. I ended up with a childhood memory of one of my bully cousins taking money from me and then making me swear that I wouldn't tell on him. I found forgiveness and while it was a somewhat intense process it didn't feel like it shook me to the core. But when I finished the process the bothersome pain that would hurt in my neck and shoulders was gone.

At first I believed it was just that this was the last process and I would be heading back to Randy's. Then I thought it's probably because I was sleeping in a different bed. When I took the long drive back to the airport and my neck didn't start hurting I figured it was because of the rental car. I conveniently forgot that it hurt on the drive in. I made every excuse I could for the pain being gone, but six months later when it still had not returned, I decided it must have been the forgiveness.

I now had a personal experience with the Journey. If only this could work as well for Nancy.

Over the next few years I would meet many people who abandoned this treatment after only one or two processes. I have personally found that it often takes more than a few to get to the root cause of an issue. I have also found many others like myself, who have had miraculous results.

It has been my experience that while having an immediate change in a health condition is rare, the natural healing process of the body can and does happen over a normal time frame. The process will also repair the outlook of the recipient in a permanent manner.

When I returned home I was eager to share the Journey processes with Nancy. The first time we tried it Nancy had some difficulty with feeling her emotions, but as time went on this became easier. She began to feel better with the processes, but the pain continued. Also, part of doing the work was swapping processes. I would facilitate for her then she would facilitate for me.

After several months of this she let me know that it was becoming more painful for her to speak. This was a concern. The issue was that there was more talking going on when she was in the process. If she became unable to speak out loud it would present some challenges for me to facilitate her process properly, and she would not receive the added benefits that speaking the words gives to the power of the process.

She was okay for now and I knew I was projecting the worst. I needed to change my outlook. Help was needed for both of us and Nancy decided that the place to get it would be at a major medical center that specialized in cancer and that also had a Holistic Alternative Medicine wing. There happened to be one just down the road.

Seeking competent medical advice is always suggested as a first priority for any medical condition. Our decisions were based on a complete understanding of Nancy's condition and the pursuit of options that would give her the best chance of survival with a consideration for quality of life. We also understood one thing above all else. We don't know how much we don't know.

Chapter 11

Sunday May 6, 2012, 11:15 a.m.

I told Dr. Edelman, "If you haven't noticed I'm one of those positive thinking glass half full sorts of guys like Zig Ziglar. As Ziglar so eloquently stated, "I'm the guy that would go after Moby Dick in a rowboat and put tartar sauce on the seat." If she didn't die back there in the ER, she's going to stay for a while.

He smiled at that, and then slowly walked out. It was clear we were done talking.

Before I let people in I explained to everyone how your face looked and how you were on so many machines and that even though you could breathe on your own; they had you on a ventilator. I hoped they wouldn't be as scared when they went in to see you; or at least they would understand what all the machines were for. A lot of people showed up to visit. I let them in two at a time while I sat quietly by and kept praying and watching over you. I felt in control, but I was scared.

What I didn't know at this time was they did CPR on you for about twenty minutes, trying to get your heart to beat again. I found that out a lot later. I was glad I didn't know at the time.

MD ANDERSON–2009

Nancy's pain began getting worse, and her ability to swallow was getting more difficult. These were things she hid quite well from me until we started with the Journey. She asked for a referral to one of the biggest and most advanced cancer centers in Texas. It was called MD Anderson. At first I thought it was about getting a second opinion. I figured anything we might hear would probably just reflect what her doctor had already discovered but sometimes it's best to seek alternate views, or to look at the same situation with new eyes. As it turned out, she had another reason.

Nancy was enthusiastic about going and hearing what they had to say. She had continued with her mostly organic no wheat, no gluten, high-vegetable diet. As far as we could tell everything had gone on as a no growth.

I had heard that this hospital had given hope to so many that just arriving here made them feel like everything was going to be okay. I spoke with one woman whose husband was there for his final round of chemotherapy. She said that when she walked through the doors she felt a wave of relief, like just being here was going to heal her husband. However, that morning we did not feel that same kind of relief we were seeking.

Our appointments that first morning were for our team leader, blood work, and CAT scan. All the meetings and tests took about two hours. The waiting time in between each appointment added up to about four hours. Every specialist we saw had a waiting room and every waiting room was full. Every wait gave us the opportunity to reflect on that feeling we had when we first came in and helped us to hone in on putting a name to it. At the end of the first day we knew why all those people in the waiting rooms were called patients. It required a lot of patience just to get through the day.

The second morning we once again started with the records people, then the dentist, the oncologist, and X-rays–lots and lots of X-rays. We also did a lot of walking and waiting. We realized that we would be seeing the records people first each day as they would give us our schedule as planned by our team leader. I'll call her Dr. Smith.

She would review everything the other doctors found and recommend and create a plan that would give Nancy the best opportunity for survival. So far no one mentioned the alternative medicine wing.

On our third day we went to records, and then we were sent to have more blood drawn. After that it was time to see our team leader, Dr. Smith. She was very matter of fact with all she had to say.

"Nancy, you have adenoid cystic carcinoma. There is no cure. Your best choice of treatment is radiation to shrink the tumors, and then surgery. This is for the two tumors below your tongue. The risks are severe bone damage from the radiation, and with the removal of the tumors you will lose your ability to speak or swallow. To eat we would insert an abdominal feeding tube. There are also four tumors in your lungs. Two of them are too close to the heart for us to treat with radiation, and surgery is not recommended for them for the same reason. The other two we would treat with a combination of radiation and chemotherapy. This could give you an optimistic three years of life."

Both of us were completely shocked. The words, *four tumors in your lungs*, kept playing over and over again. Had these tumors been there all along? We were both completely paralyzed.

I looked at Dr. Smith and said, "Could you give us a minute?"

"Yes, take all the time you need."

"We'll need about thirty years." I said.

She left us in the room, and I held Nancy's hand.

"What do you want to do?" I said.

"I'm not doing any of this," Nancy said. "We still have one more doctor to see."

"Which one?" I asked.

"The pain doctor. It would be nice if someone here could offer me something that actually made me feel better."

I held Nancy close. Sometimes there is nothing that can be said with words that can convey your message. When Nancy finally said it was okay, I called Dr. Smith back in. We told her our decision on the treatment and asked to see the pain specialist.

"I understand," she said.

Then we were on our way to our last appointment in the main hospital. For the first time since we arrived, we understood the feeling that had overcome us as we walked through the front doors. It was dread: The feeling that everything is hopeless.

Surprisingly, the wait for the pain doctor was remarkably short. Less than twenty minutes after arriving we were in his office. He explained what could be done, basically telling us that the medication was a tradeoff of numbing the pain without sacrificing too much consciousness. He then gave us the preferred starting drug for reducing pain. Nancy put it in her purse. She had tried it before without success. She would try it again, but not right now. There was still unfinished business.

At the end of our consultation Nancy asked, “I have heard there is an alternative treatment wing here at the hospital. I would like to be referred.”

The doctor said it was up to our team leader to initiate the referral, but he would pass along her request. Before we left the hospital that day we had our appointment for the alternative medicine wing.

MD Anderson had floors of buildings each dedicated to one science. They had entire buildings dedicated to specific types of cancer. It was truly impressive the dedication they had to improving one’s chance of success at surviving cancer. We could not wait to get to the section of the hospital that was solely dedicated to treatment that was of a more divine nature.

We knew the alternative medicine wing was a place where belief was born of knowing our divine potential, as opposed to what could be seen through a microscope. And we would be there in the morning, because no one else could help us, and it seemed this was the only way to get referred.

I knew where Nancy’s real faith was; it was here with the people who believed in the power of belief. She had decided that long ago. I knew where my real faith was. I knew that before Nancy and I decided to marry. We were at a place where the only thing conventional medicine could offer us was time, and that was offered with no guarantees, and at the expense of her voice and her ability to eat. The treatment might well shorten her life. She had to ask herself how she wanted to spend the time she had left. All medical avenues were exhausted. There was only one place left to look at this medical center. It was the place where the hopeless go.

In terms of alternative treatment or supplemental treatment there are many, many, options: Nutrition, exercise, yoga, acupressure, acupuncture, massage therapy, Reiki, hypnotherapy, meditation, chiropractic treatment, homeopathic, thought field therapy, Chi Gong, and now the process work we were using with The Journey. These are just the ones I can name off of the top of my head. I am sure there are more. Imagine how surprised we were to find the "Alternative Treatment" wing to be little more than eight rooms. This included the bathrooms. I guess they figured if it was that good, and it wanted more space, it would manifest it on its own.

We entered, and after checking in we were given a packet with meditation CDs and a brief explanation of what was offered. All that was offered at that time was a Reiki class, and we decided to take it.

When we left the main hospital that day, we had been given a great deal of surprising news that offered little hope, until we met Ray. Ray had only one thing going for him: without the help of the medical profession he had cured himself of cancer. He was our Reiki teacher. It was easy to listen to Ray. He spoke from personal experience, and he believed every word he said. Still, I am not sure if I could have listened to him had I not had the experiences that led me to him. He had been told his situation was hopeless. He had a few months left, and there was nothing more they could do.

"The key word," Ray said, "is '*they*.' There was nothing more 'they' could do. I heard what they said and then realized there was still a lot that 'I' could do. I chose Reiki as my primary treatment. So let's get started and you can see what I did that removed the cancer from this body, eight years ago."

During his class we learned the skills we would need to perform the treatment. We did the treatment at least once each day while we were staying in Houston and about once a day as part of our routine for as long as Nancy believed it could do her some good. Meeting Ray opened up a lot of doors to other treatments used besides experimental medication to extend lives or entirely eliminate cancer from their bodies. Nancy would try many of these healing modalities.

New discoveries are coming out every day about the power

of belief. Ray believed that Reiki, was what would work for him, and it did. Others believe that radiation or chemotherapy is the answer to eliminating cancer and for some that belief works. For me, the most important question to ask was, what does Nancy believe?

I believe most of us put a lot of faith in the ones who spend their lives trying to benefit those who are sick or injured. I believe most doctors feel helpless when all they have learned fails, and I cannot imagine living with that burden. Nancy spent most of her life putting her faith in the knowledge and learning of things that could be measured and seen. At the same time she was studying the powers of faith and belief. No matter what the choice, in the end we all meet the same fate. It's just a question of which gives you the life you desire, or at least the life that's better for you.

I knew from experience that feeling bad would do more to worsen a health condition than most anything else. I could also see that even with meeting Ray, Nancy felt discouraged and confused as to why there was so much tumor growth that she had not recognized. It was time to do something fantastic and do it now. It was time to step up. The problem was I was feeling as bad as she was. Then I remembered the birthday week Nancy gave me when we first met, and how special I felt.

Chapter 12

Monday, May 7, 2012, about 4:30 a.m. It was your second day at the hospital.

You started to wake up. Our nurse, Edward, came in right away, and said that your body was acclimating to one of the two sedatives you were on. Before they increased the dose to keep you asleep he asked you, "Nancy can you please squeeze my hand?"

He immediately placed two fingers in your palm, and you squeezed. I told him, "Ask her something harder."

He said, "Nancy, can you give me a thumbs up?"

You immediately placed your thumb in the air. Edward looked at me, smiled and said, "That is a very good sign."

BUCKET LIST: VACATION TO MOAB, UTAH, AND CANYONLANDS–2010

There was something that Nancy had always wanted to do. Something she had not shared with me. Something I had no interest in whatsoever. She wanted to go to Arches National Park and see Delicate Arch. She also wanted to go to Canyonlands National Park and Canyon De Chelly, pronounced (Shay). She had wanted to do this for many years, and after our vacation to MD Anderson she shared this with me for the first time.

We were planning to take a vacation to celebrate Nancy's retirement. This would be the perfect opportunity and I was excited beyond belief about this trip. It was what she deserved. We had a new car, we had time, and we had the money. As usual, Nancy made the plans. I had a few things going on at the time with work but sometimes you have to let things go to do what's really important.

I had noticed that Nancy had trouble swallowing rice. She started to avoid it. I also noticed that she was once again losing weight. Her spirits seemed bright but there was a sense of urgency in the timing of this vacation. I had just finished a big job and was ready to start on another when the decision to go was made. Even though I thought it would be nice to have the fee for this next job in hand I put it off without a thought.

When I was younger I was on a job that ended up taking longer than expected and canceled a trip to see my family in New England. As a result of the cancellation it took me over a year to get back up there to see them. All of us were disappointed. It turned out to be a bad decision, both business and personal.

There was nothing that Nancy wanted to do that I was willing to put off, even for a day. We had looked over the edge of the cliff at the waterfall. We were choosing life.

Our day arrived; with the car packed we set our intention to adventure, and with love of life in our hearts we drove off into the sunrise. It was amazing. I took a picture of the dashboard as we drove out of the driveway. The radio said snow patrol (It was the name of the group playing on the radio). We decided it was a metaphor for the coolest vacation ever, and we were going on it. Nancy pulled out of the driveway pointed the car toward the horizon, and headed us toward adventure, all the while holding onto one thought; things can always get better.

When we arrived at the Santa Fe Inn and checked in, we were pleased to find our room looked just like the picture. It was rustic Southwest in yellows and browns, with a small fridge and couch. It was perfect for quiet evenings after a long day of walking, looking at churches, and buying Indian jewelry that I seldom see Indians wearing. We would be here for two nights, which would be just right, as you can only look at churches for so long before someone will ask you to join.

Our first evening there we went to a chocolate shop we had read about that had the purest chocolate, with the least amount of manipulation. It was not the sweet sugary chocolate that is found in confectionary shops, it was the food of the Gods. Both Nancy and I thought this ought to be enough to cure anything. But all it cured was our chocolate craving. The next day we went to the oldest church in America, and another church that had a spiral staircase that defied the laws of physics.

These things may have meant more to us at a different time in our lives. Now we looked at them as things that had lasted beyond normal years, but no longer served the purpose they were created for. It was now their age that was exalted above the primary reason they were built in the first place. We found that sad.

After that we decided to go to some of the galleries. While walking past a gallery we found a clay tiger holding a drum dressed in ceremonial Indian leather. It was about twelve inches tall and had a baby tiger poking its head out of the clothing at the center of the tiger's chest.

"That's amazing," Nancy said.

I remembered her chosen name at Warrior Retreat was Little Tiger.

"Let's see how much it is," I said, as I walked with her into the gallery.

We spoke to Allen, the owner of the gallery, who told us about the person who made the tiger. It was a prominent artist who lived in the area and this piece was available for only eight hundred dollars. We went back to look at it again I could tell that Nancy really wanted it, yet something was holding her back.

"If you want this I can get it right now," I said. "We can have it shipped to our house or to a local gallery in Fort Worth."

"I think it's wonderful David, but I don't want it that bad. It's beautiful but...." Nancy's voice trailed off. "I'm just not ready to buy it."

Allen placed it back in the front window. I figured it would be gone by the time we left so I did the next best thing. I took a picture of it. Nancy could look at it whenever she wanted, and be free of the guilt of spending a lot of cash.

I thought about this a lot; was she trying to save money

for me, or was she really not that interested? The real issue of course, wasn't with her. It was my reaction to her decision. I was the one who couldn't let it go.

With our spirits high, the next day we started for Utah. Along the way we decided to take a detour to Four Corners. The Four Corners area is where the four states: New Mexico, Colorado, Utah, and Arizona all meet; this is the only place where four states come together at one point. Sadly, the whole place was developed before satellite technology revealed that the place marked, is not accurate. We didn't care. Our spirit was there. The thought that we could be at a place where we had so many choices was too good to pass up.

If only we could believe our lives are like that. We could just take one step and change our state of being. Over here I'm a cancer patient, but take one step to the right and I'm a cancer survivor. Take one more I'm my ideal weight; but go too far and I'm back to being a cancer patient. In life we all have choices each day and it is as easy as stepping over a line on the ground to change our decision. I just wished I could help Nancy make up her mind.

We looked down at our feet where the four corners came together, and decided what state we wanted to be in: cancer survivor. We went to the car and headed to Moab. Moab was one of the two reasons for this vacation, although I didn't know it at the time.

We had made reservations at a bed and breakfast in Moab, called Sunflower Hill. We had a suite that was all by itself between the main building and a building that was used as a common area. This common area was also used as the main dining area where breakfast would be served. We got there pretty late so we went right to bed, letting the cozy, old-fashioned peacefulness of the room carry us away.

The next morning we went to breakfast and we had a terrific choice of foods from waffles to fresh fruit along with oatmeal and other cereals. They had at least four different kinds of bread that looked homemade. I went right for the waffles and Nancy hit the fruit and oatmeal.

About three bites into the oatmeal Nancy started to choke. She was coughing trying to dislodge some food that had caught in her throat. It took almost a full minute for her to get it out. I was very concerned to say the least. I could see that she could breathe, but her face was very red. When she was calmed and had a chance to catch her breath I asked if she was okay.

"I had trouble swallowing the oatmeal. It got caught the same way the rice did. I may have to stop eating it," she said.

I told Nancy, "This is a different kind than we have at home, so maybe it's just this kind of oatmeal."

"I don't think I want to risk it," she said. "How are you?"

"I was a little scared too. Are you going to eat something else?"

"Yes, I'm going to finish the fruit, and have some yogurt."

"Sounds good, I'll have some too."

At this point inside I was getting more concerned. I knew the coughing caused her a lot of pain that would not just go away because the coughing subsided. Still she acted as if everything were normal. I knew this was something she had a lot of practice doing. I knew it because I had been the same until I met her.

She helped me be honest, and I trusted her to do the same. I gave her time to let me know how she felt. I was patient, but it was distracting for me to want to look after her and at the same time see what she saw in this place filled with natural wonders. It was necessary for me to be present for her to truly get everything she could out of this trip. I needed for her to share her appreciation of all we saw.

We finished breakfast and went to the room to get ready for a day at Arches National Park. I wasn't sure what we would see there. I hoped the sights would take her mind off what had just happened. I hoped it would take my mind off what just happened, too. I knew there were arches and other rock formations but I couldn't tell you what they looked like. I did know that Nancy was very interested in the formations. When she came out to the car ready to go I couldn't imagine that this girl was the same one that had just been scared at breakfast. She was absolutely confident, excited, and ready for anything.

We entered the park and watched a film on how the arches were formed, and where they were located. We saw many arches, each one was magnificent in its own unique way, but each one had a path to it that was between one quarter- and a half-mile walk. Once we arrived at one of the arches we would spend some time taking pictures and taking in the spectacle that was there. I knew the walking was strenuous for her but she seemed to get a burst of energy at the entrance of each attraction. As we neared the end of the day I could tell Nancy was low on fuel. The last one she wanted to see was Delicate Arch. It was the reason we went to Arches National Park, and the biggest reason we went on vacation at all.

The hike to Delicate Arch was about a mile and a half one way, and climbed about 480 feet. We decided to spend some time resting at the car before we started the trail. We ate some snacks to give us some energy then started the assent. I'm not sure what it was that made this climb so difficult but I was having a tough time pushing up the hills, so I knew it was taking everything Nancy had. At one point about three quarters of the way up she stopped. She had given all she had. We needed to rest.

"I'm not sure I can make it. How much longer do you think it is?" Nancy asked.

Just then, a man was coming down the hill, so I asked him.

"Excuse me, how much farther is it to the top?"

"Not too much farther," he said. "When you get to the top of this rise it's less than a quarter mile."

"Thanks, we appreciate it. It's been a tough day, and this is our last arch."

"Good luck," he said. With that he continued down the hill.

I looked at Nancy and said. "I know you don't want to miss this and if I need to carry you I can."

Nancy smiled at the thought and got up. "I'll make it. I just needed to rest a little more."

A few minutes later we were once again on our way. Soon she would be rejuvenated and filled with excitement about this place, and I would be the one who didn't want to move.

At the top of the hill the path led us around the side of a small mountain. The path was narrow by my standards. It was less than three feet wide. On my right was the side of the mountain and on my left was a 100-foot cliff. There were no handrails, or anything that would prevent me from hurling off it should I stumble, and there were people going in both directions. I now knew I had a fear of heights. I never really knew how disturbing it was until I was walking on that path. Lucky for me in the two lanes of traffic I was on the inside, but what was I to do on the way down when I would be on the outside?

This treacherous part of the path was less than a hundred feet in length so we got through it quickly. When we got to the top we found ourselves on the ridge of this narrow mountaintop. To one side was the cliff, to the other side was a drop off that was like a steep roof, a very steep roof. It looked like once you started to slide down you wouldn't be able to stop until you got to the bottom. The bottom was a long way down. I seemed to miss that ahead of us was Delicate Arch.

I had seen this formation on calendars, and book covers, even travel brochures. I understood why Nancy wanted to see it. It was late in the day, the sun was setting, and the moon was on the rise. I realized what she wanted was a picture of the moon inside the arch. I could see photographers set up, most of them in one area, to get such a picture. They were on the steep slope. I was not going there.

I noticed others walking over to the arch to get their picture taken in it. The walk over to the arch involved being on the slope; I was not going there either. I looked around and although the ridge was mostly flat and about fifteen feet across, I was getting dizzy. It didn't help that there was a strong wind blowing and no matter where I turned it seemed as if it was pushing me off. I climbed on a large rock and closed my eyes.

Nancy knew something was wrong, and came over to sit with me. I let her know how I was feeling and that I was having difficulty with heights. She sat with me a while until I felt better and asked if she could walk around. I handed her the camera and placed my head in my folded arms. I found it very difficult to watch her walk around up there. I also felt very stupid for being paralyzed by a fear that was in my mind.

Nancy walked around for a while as I sat. It seemed like we were there a long time, but I don't know. She came back and sat down beside me. I took the camera and took some pictures of the arch, then of the drop offs that were on either side of me. I looked at Nancy. We may never get back here I thought. This could be the only time we get to see this. With this thought firmly entrenched in my consciousness I said to my loving sweet wife, who just this morning found out she would no longer eat oatmeal, "I can't stay here much longer. I'm so sorry."

I will never forget the look of compassion she had for me at that moment.

"It's okay David. We can go if you want to. I've seen what I came to see."

"Thanks Honey, I'm really having a hard time."

"Will you be okay getting around the mountain?"

"I hope so."

As we started down the path all I could think about was the fact that if someone was coming up, I would have to be on the cliff side of the path. The thought almost completely overwhelmed me. When we neared the bend I could see that no one was coming toward us, so I hugged the mountainside all the way around until we were once again descending the hill, safely on our way back to the car.

I have never felt so much shame as on that day at Delicate Arch. Although Nancy never said anything, I knew what she wanted. I had seen pictures of the moon in the arch. I took a picture of others standing in the arch. I let fear stop me from giving her the full experience of a lifelong dream. I thought about her in the raft up in Maine when she wanted to be in the safer, ten-person raft, and I insisted on the smaller one, for more excitement. She seemed fearless, although I knew that wasn't the case. I knew something needed to change in me and change fast. Tomorrow we were headed to Canyonlands, and I suspected that the opportunity to face this fear would once again present itself.

CANYONLANDS

Canyonlands National Park consists of over 500 square miles of canyons. We would be primarily interested in the overlooks around the canyons. Because of the size of the park we would first view the overlooks from the north entrance then proceed to the entrance farthest south. We were heading to the rim of a spectacle the likes of which we had never seen.

Our first stop was an outlook that was located at the center finger with a view that would look toward the central source where all three fingers were connected. It was a magnificent view. Like Arches National Park there were no safety rails. We could walk to the ridge of the canyon and look out over a 200-foot drop to the first level of the canyon floor. I was able to get within six feet of the edge without my palms sweating, but this was still close enough to get the full expansive magnificent view.

After looking for a while I backed away to get some balance and look around at the other formations and vegetation there. When I went back toward the ledge Nancy was sitting on it with her legs dangling off. If she lost a shoe there would be no way to retrieve it. It was the bravest thing I've ever seen anyone do. I took a picture, and then quietly approached from the side far enough away so as not to startle her. I knew if she started to fall that my fear would keep me from trying to save her.

Up until then, I had always thought of myself as fearless. I could walk a two-story house roof with a forty-five degree pitch with no problem. I couldn't imagine where this fear came from, and at the time I had no idea what to do about it. It was keeping me from sharing Nancy's experience and filling me with not just fear, but extreme disappointment. I felt I was failing her in a way that I could never make right. I knew the chances of me ever getting to this place with her again were almost zero.

Nancy looked at me and smiled. I walked over as close as I dared and she let me know there was a small outcropping of rocks several feet below. If she had fallen off she would have landed there, and hopefully not fallen any further. She felt safe.

I was the one who was scared. I was scared of death. I was the one playing it safe. I turned away from an experience I would never get again. I realized I was afraid to live also. Where can I run when I fear death and life?

A while later I asked what she was doing going out on the edge like that? She said, "I was talking to God."

"Was it necessary for you to get right in his face?"

She laughed at that. I never asked her what she was talking to God about, but years later I would ask God about it.

We had several more stops on this dream vacation, this bucket list of things that Nancy most wanted to do, but the most important things were behind us. We had already discovered things in ourselves that were both beautiful and hard to look at. We would use these discoveries to live more fully, more completely, and more closely to one another.

The thing Nancy did for me on this vacation was to show me the world through her eyes. When I looked, I found more beauty than I had ever seen before. I also saw my fears, and how my fears held me back. This was my regret: That I couldn't give Nancy the fullest most complete experience possible. On the final drive back home I made a decision not to ever let my fear stop me from living a full life with this beautiful woman who was now sitting beside me, and most of all I would not let my fear keep her from fully experiencing life as she was choosing to live it.

Nancy made a vow too; she vowed that just being at the canyons and arches was okay. She would enjoy the experience of her choice and enjoy the company of someone she loved despite his fears. It was an amazing act of forgiveness and acceptance on her part. She allowed me my comfort zone and helped me release my guilt. It wasn't about compromise so much as about accepting each other as we were. We both had limitations and as she recognized that it was not an imposition for me to eat her chosen diet, she was pleased to be able to give me the gift of us sharing our experience while respecting the caution I felt at the time. But hey, things can always get better.

Chapter 13

Monday, May 7, 2012, 8:30 a.m.

This morning, Dr. Weston, then each of the nurses who tended to you in the ER yesterday, visited you one at a time. The ER was separate from the hospital and ICU, so the visit was not part of normal procedure. Each one who came in told you how strong you were, and they were so happy you were doing so well.

I found it really touching that they cared enough to visit on their own time like that. It was pointed out to me that this was not normal procedure. It always amazes me how a loving presence can bring out the best in us. Even with you being unconscious, you had obviously touched all of these medical professionals who had not given up on you, and I knew you would not give up on them.

THE DEATH EXPERIENCE–2011

In my mind it was time to eliminate the fear that held me back at Canyonlands. How could I help Nancy face her fears without me stepping up and facing mine? We discussed taking the full program that The Journey offered. She told me she couldn't travel as much as would be required, but suggested I get the material and share it with her. At that point she had attended five of the programs offered. I would bring her the rest.

Nancy and I embraced facing our fears. I would attend two, two-week long retreats: No- Ego retreat, and the Practitioner retreat. This would give me a more complete arsenal of whatever was available to face Nancy's and my own condition head on. The first was, "No Ego."

The most significant thing happened the first day. I was paired up with the lead Practitioner and we were sitting knee to knee, eye to eye. Her name was Bet. She asked me, "David, what is your highest intention for this week?"

I answered honestly with a voice full of emotion and eyes wet with tears, "I want to clear my fears, so that I can save my wife's life."

I believe Bet fully sensed the depth of my commitment. I then asked Bet, "What is your highest intention for this week?"

Her reply, filled with emotion and tears was, "I want to do all I can to help you clear your fears, so you can save your wife's life."

While I will not go into the details of the retreat she was true to her word, as was everyone I met, whether professional, volunteer, or participant.

Next was the Practitioner retreat. This would be the last retreat I would need to attend to complete my studies. I knew there was several processes I still needed to learn, and I was confident in my ability to be open and receptive. I also knew that every person here was as committed as I was, not only to our own personal growth, but to our partner's growth as well.

There comes a time in the lives of many of us where we make a friend of the idea of death. Perhaps we accept its inevitability, or perhaps we look forward to it when life becomes too painful. For me it was because of my relationship with Nancy.

I have always believed that I was guided to my highest good. I knew there was a good chance that Nancy was going to die as a result of her cancer. I knew that I was her primary caregiver and that I would always be that. I also trusted that whatever I was led to do would be the right thing to do, and that myself and all others involved would be okay. I had this in mind when I entered one of the last Journey processes on the fourth day of the retreat.

My partner was Doug. He had been my roommate on the last retreat. "Doug," I said, "I have set an intention for this process and I want you to promise me that no matter what happens you will not touch or try to rescue me in any way. Are you willing to comply with my request?"

"Yes," he said giving me a sideways sort of look that suggested a level of concern about what he has just agreed to do. "What is your intention for this process?" he asked.

"I want to experience death."

As Doug stared at me, his face remaining expressionless, his mouth wordless, I could imagine the thoughts that were pouring through his mind. I am about to be the only person on the planet who has ever had someone die during a Journey Process. I wonder if they will believe me when I'm standing over his lifeless body saying, really, he said not to touch him or do anything....

I had made a request that may have been unprecedented, but I felt it was necessary and for my highest good. I knew he was the only one who could do this with me. I just didn't know if he knew it.

After several long moments that seemed to stretch into hours, he blinked and said, "Okay, are you ready to begin?"

We both offered a prayer for this process to reveal all that I had requested, and for both of us to benefit from the experience.

The Journey I was engaging in would lead me down a staircase and through a door to meet my mentor. I would then climb into a transport of some sort and go to a place in my body where a memory was stored. At this point I would do what is called a drop through from the feelings that were here until I felt Source energy, or God's presence. I would then wash up through the emotions to the strongest feeling and there would find the experience I requested.

As Doug began to lead me through the process I was surprised at how calm and assured he was. This was just what I needed to get the most out of my Journey. When I arrived at the place where I met my mentor I almost laughed when he turned out to be a character from a series of horror movies. The character's name was John, and his famous line was, "Live or Die, make your choice."

Doug led me through the rest of the process through the part where I arrive at the scene where I have an issue that needs understanding and forgiveness.

The scene opens:

I am at a funeral and John, my mentor, is dressed like the Ghost of Christmas future from the Charles Dickens book, *A Christmas Carol.* Like in the book, he points without saying a word to the casket, which is at the front of the room. I almost laugh at the predictability of the scene and I shake my head at how easy it is to walk to the casket. I look inside and freeze in my tracks. The breath leaves my body and my eyes fill with tears. I'm not in the casket; Nancy is.

For a minute I can't move. I can't turn my head or even close my eyes. Even now I can barely describe the feeling of complete helplessness, as I look down and see the person I have loved more than life itself laying there before me. I don't know what to do; then quite suddenly I feel Nancy's spirit behind me. Her touch frees me to move and I turn to look at her, and she asks me one question. "Do you understand?"

My mind is spinning as I try to make sense of what is happening, and suddenly, like someone took a sledgehammer and busted my heart out of a stone tomb I understand. I say to this lovely divine being that has shared my life for the last four and a half years, "You go on. So you have not experienced death, only life. For me to experience death, I have to be the one left behind."

She smiles at me, like a slow student who finally gets it. I feel warmth in my chest that turns to light until that's all I can see. She is a part of me now, and I know she always will be. For the first time in my life I can find no fear in my being. There is only peace.

I feel like I'm finished but John asks me if there is some forgiveness that needs to take place. "Not yet John," I say. "If Nancy dies, then I will need to forgive both her and myself."

John tells me "Forgiveness is giving in advance."

I turn to see Nancy once again standing with me, and say, "If this is our choice, I will support you in your decision. If you decide to live and you are disfigured or handicapped in any way, I will be there with you to love and support you as well. All forgiveness is here. I love the being that I know you are, and the form you choose will not change that."

Nancy smiles at me like I'm a quick learner. The whole scene disappears. Only John and I are left.

We finish the process easily and I thank Doug for being a true and trusting friend. I'm now ready to finish the week then go home. I know why I came to the Journey. I have received a tremendous gift. I feel like I can be whoever Nancy needs as she continues her life with me.

The one thing I can't avoid is my greatest fear; it's not her death or even mine, it's my life if I have to go on without her. I know if I spend all my time trying to avoid the inevitable I will miss the blessed experience of life with her, and leave this place unfulfilled. I know I need help. I have worked with others who have suffered a death loss, and even with the experience I have now had, I know if Nancy decided to leave before me, it will still be more than I am able to handle.

I walk outside and sit on a short stone wall to reflect on what I have just experienced. As I'm sitting there I notice a woman about my age coming from the process room. She notices me and comes over. "Mind if I sit down?" she asks.

"Not at all," I say.

"I don't know why, but I feel like I'm supposed to talk to you. My name's Lawny."

"Hi Lawny, I'm David."

"Nice to meet you David, so how was your process?"

I told Lawny all about it, watching her eyes widen at the part where I asked to experience death, and watching her eyes moisten with tears, at the part where Nancy was the one in the casket.

"That's quite a request; to experience death. I think I know why I'm supposed to talk to you," she said. "My husband died last year after a long battle with cancer."

She told me how he was a good and loving man, and how they had two daughters together. She loved him very much, and life without him was difficult because she missed him. Memories of him often occupied her thoughts, and her daughters often spent time talking of the wonderful memories they shared. It gave them comfort. It was after that she shared what I most needed to hear.

"When his death was near, the girls and I were there with him in the room, and at the moment of his death we could feel his presence all around us. It surrounded us and filled us and we knew he was okay. We cried and stayed with him and we washed him as we waited for the funeral home to take his body. It was so beautiful."

All I could say as I sat there with my eyes filled with tears was, "Thank you Lawny, thank you so much for sharing this. I'm sure we will talk again."

After a hug we both went to our rooms to reflect on the grace we had experienced. It was truly a blessing that we were both able to be led to help each other; me with the possibility of losing the one I loved, and her having recently experienced such a loss. Two sides of what could be a very similar experience. It seemed I had been given a new support system.

I reasoned that my willingness to experience death might be somewhat disturbing to Nancy so I decided not to mention it unless she asked. She seldom asked about my processes other than if I had been able to forgive, but if she did ask, honesty would prevail. I emailed Nancy that night and let her know the process went well and I was able to work through a fear I had been working on. I also told her I had met Lawny and that her husband had cancer, but did not survive. I let her know that Lawny had said that her husband would not do any Journey work or any alternative treatment for his condition, but she felt it might have helped.

Nancy replied to my email the next morning and wished me well in the upcoming work. She also let me know that during one of her Chi Gong sessions something inside of her changed. Her tolerance of the pain she was experiencing was lessened by half. She assured me that her pain had not increased she just had less tolerance for it.

I found this news not only disturbing but distracting. I texted her to see if I should come home right away, but she assured me that everything was okay, and it would be to both of our benefits for me to finish the retreat. After several more emails and texts we confirmed the decision for me to stay. But making the decision did not keep me from being distracted. I felt I had been gone too long and I missed her terribly. This effort was about me having this experience to help her to heal. If she didn't make it, how was I going to feel about being gone so long?

On the second to last day we had what was called a Life's Purpose process. This was not about knowing what kind of vocation one would have, so much as what our core talent was. For some it might be to bring joy to those around us, or it could be to promote healing or even to bring clarity for others, and some might be teachers. When I took my process I found that what I could do best was see the good in all that was around me. Perhaps it was what was needed for Nancy. I wanted to be a healing presence in her life, and I could do that, but I could also see her position and love her even if she chose to give up.

On the last day we did the Life's Purpose process again; for me the results were the same, but it taught me to make sure when I did this with Nancy to repeat the process the next day. In all, on my return Nancy would have the opportunity to experience both the Designer process and then Life's Purpose process. Both of which would be new for her. My hope was that the Designer process would help her discover the cause of her cancer, and the life's purpose would give her a direction and some excitement about the things she might want to do with her life. With both of us making these discoveries together I felt we would be able to grow even closer than we were.

At one time in my life I believed as many do, that if I loved someone enough they would automatically love me back. I also thought that love meant possession of the object of my affection. With Nancy and me it was different.

Our bond was not based on dependency, but the desire to be intimate: To learn and contribute to each other's growth. We always wanted to be closer. We found that by sharing these processes and the experience of both of our strengths and weaknesses, then we could grow closer than either of us had ever experienced. "Into me see," this was our quest, to be transparent to the best of our ability.

Brandon gave us the gift of live music of a very spiritual nature to finish our last day. I could have hung around after and left in the morning, but the thought of spending any more time away from home was unbearable. I drove for about four hours that evening and called Nancy both when I left the retreat and when I got to the hotel. It would be a ten-hour drive back to our home.

"I'm safe for the night Honey," I said over the phone. "I'll be up early and should be getting in early tomorrow night. I've missed you so much, but I'm excited about you having these new Journey processes."

"I've missed you too, Honey Bunny, I can't wait to see you, but please drive safe. We can start the process work the day after you get back," Nancy said.

After we said our goodbyes I immediately went to bed and set my alarm for five a.m. It would be good to be home, and begin what I hoped would be a road to a speedy recovery.

I was up before the alarm as usual, and I packed and got on the road right away. On all the other retreats I was anxious to get home, but this time because of the pain tolerance thing I was more determined than usual. I had even considered driving through last night, although I knew Nancy would be very angry about me driving that long. As it was I planned on getting home around six-thirty that evening.

I called when I was about an hour from home to let her know I was close, and how much I missed her. It helped her not to worry when I contacted her regularly on the way home. I arrived home on time and held her as if just doing so would make the pain go away. Of course it didn't but I couldn't help but wish it could. I asked how she was, and she said, "I'm doing okay tonight. I feel a lot better now that you're home."

"Me too, I missed you so much. I can't wait to let you know about everything. I really think this can help. Do you want me to do a pain process?"

"No, I'm good for now. Aren't you tired?"

"Yes but that process doesn't take long, and I want you to feel as good as you can."

"Thanks Honey Bunny, I'm all right. Why don't you sit down and I'll get you something to drink and you can rub my feet."

"Now you're talking."

Rubbing Nancy's feet always relaxed me. Just knowing she was feeling good made all my tensions go away. I loved the way her face would relax and her shoulders would soften. It let me know I was doing well. I would spend about fifteen minutes on each foot, and see how she felt. It felt good to be home with her. I had another tool in my toolbox of things that might help her heal. I could hardly wait to try it out.

We got ready for bed after that. When we both settled in we spent some time just being with each other. These were the times when we felt closest. It was just the two of us and we could shut out the rest of the world, and most importantly, what was going on inside our heads. Our minds would quiet, and we could just enjoy each other's company, two as one. It was during this time she asked me if her speech sounded different. That could only mean she felt she was losing control of her tongue. I hadn't noticed any change but the fact that she was asking took the wind out of my sails and scared me in spite of my experience of death.

Fear it would seem was something that would continue to creep up on me from time to time, especially when it came to Nancy. There was a gift in what Lawny had told me. It was that I could still know Nancy was safe and with me even if she died. I would be able to feel her presence. The question was would it be enough?

Chapter 14

Tuesday, May 8, 2012, 6:30 a.m. This is your third day in the hospital.

I decided to assist the nurses when they had to bathe you or move you in the bed. The only other thing was suctioning the tube they placed in your throat. As this was temporary I decided it was not as important for me to know. The first day of suctioning filled a basin on the wall with blood and mucous. Today you would only fill one half way. I figured this meant you were getting better.

Also, the puffiness around your face was way down. They tried putting you on just one sedative, but you started to wake up, and started bucking the ventilator so they put you back on two sedatives. They were constantly adjusting things to give you the best possible chance for a full recovery.

THE BELOVED COMMUNITY–2011

Nancy and I were always learning. Both of us had embraced studies in many directions. For me it had been the Journey, and a little bit of Peak Potentials. For Nancy it was Peak Potentials, and a little bit of Journey. After her retirement she was looking for something a little different and discovered The Beloved Community. It was started by James Twyman.

The Beloved Community is a Christian-based organization that was centered in the Divine Feminine and on the Gospel of John. Nancy investigated it and decided to enroll in their seminary program. It took her about a year to complete almost all of her studies. The only thing left was to attend a retreat. She now had a choice. She could attend the final retreat and just go home or stay after the retreat and be ordained as a minister. This was not her objective, but it could be useful to her later on.

She asked me about her being ordained one night before we went to bed. "They have a retreat that I want to attend to finish my program and an ordination ceremony afterward. It will be in Oregon if I want to go. I know I'm probably not going to do anything as a minister, but I want to know what you think about my going to the retreat and being ordained."

"I think you should. I know I'd like to go to the retreat with you if I can. As far as the ordination, you have earned the title and you may need the title later on. Being an ordained minister could open some doors for you. So what do you say?"

"Well, I think it would be fun for us to go, and maybe we could see some stuff while we're there. Crater Lake isn't too far away and neither is Ashland."

"Okay let's plan the trip and see what we can see."

We broke out the maps, but as usual it was Nancy that had something in mind. First she showed me pictures of a beautiful little bed and breakfast there that was near several waterfalls that were easy to walk to. It was about forty miles from Crater Lake, but it was all highway so we thought the drive should be easy. We could get there the day before and go to the coast, and get a hotel near the retreat, and because it was late summer the weather would be pleasant. We made our hotel and our plane reservations and reserved a rental car. With our sights on my first trip to the Northwest, and Nancy's first trip to Oregon, we confidently moved on.

There was only one thing that seemed to be an issue. Nancy was having more trouble swallowing. She was eating smoothies and protein shakes, but no solid food. It had become too painful and too difficult to chew or manipulate solid food in her mouth. Talking had become painful as well. Several weeks after returning from the last Journey retreat she told me she could no longer facilitate Journey processes for me. There was too much speaking involved. Her voice had begun to slur. She could still talk but it was getting harder to understand her. We decided it was time to limit her words as best we could.

Upon arrival in Oregon we set our sights to getting to the hotel near the retreat that preceded the ordination. On the way to the hotel we would stick our feet in the Pacific Ocean. This would be our third time and although every time was in the summer, the water was always freezing cold to us. As we passed through a seaside town we found our way to the beach and did the deed; me getting my foot all the way in and her getting a tiny portion of her toe wet. This was our official business that was always tended to. After that it was just about finding something Nancy could eat and continuing our drive.

The best we found was an Asian restaurant that had some soup that we had pureed. It still turned out to be difficult but at least she had some calories. She was getting her vitamins in the morning smoothies so I wasn't worried about that. What I was concerned about was the fact that she weighed only about ninety pounds, so the idea of her missing any meal was frightening to me. I knew by the time we got to the hotel it would be late, but at least the protein shake would be substantial.

We found our hotel with ease, and after some quick shopping and mixing, I had an evening shake ready for Nancy. We found ourselves exhausted after the day's travel, and headed straight to bed.

In the morning after a quick breakfast we took the short drive to the retreat house. The house was secluded with a long driveway that led to the site. There were small cabins set up about one every hundred feet, where we would stay. Of the six or so that they had, only two had electricity. We had one of the two. The cabins were located along a walking path that one might take to relax or meditate. There were prayers set up along the path for spiritual deepening, as well as places to rest. Also along the path there was a large two-story geodesic dome tent, and a 200- square-foot deck that was suspended by chains about twenty feet off the ground. The place was amazing.

The main house had the sanctuary where we would meet for our instruction. During our introduction session, we were placed in groups that were named after arch angels. I was in group Michael, and Nancy was assigned to Gabriel. The groups were then given assignments to cook a meal or clean up afterwards. We were all given two assignments each, one to cook and one to clean. I found myself volunteering on Nancy's team as well as my own. It wasn't so much that she couldn't do what was necessary, she was just considerably weaker than everyone knew and that would slow down preparation; also her meals would need special preparation time as well.

When I reflected on this I felt that although it might have been what Nancy preferred, it robbed the others of the opportunity to be patient and understanding, something they probably would have easily accomplished. There was a level of dishonesty about it even though my intentions were what I considered generous. I was there to support Nancy in a way that she wanted. The thing I forgot, was to ask what she wanted before I did it.

The retreat went well and at the end we all felt deeply moved by our experiences. It was now time for the ordination. This ceremony was very sacred. Nancy, and the others who would be ordained, were all dressed in white, as were those who would perform the ordination. After opening prayers, the initiates would take turns having their feet washed by their mentors. It was a reflection of how Jesus treated the apostles before the last supper. This was followed by the placing of the stole on each one and announcing their title as a Peace Minister in the Beloved Community. There was a deep reverence for this, and I felt blessed just to be there.

When it was done I asked Nancy if she felt any different than she felt before the ceremony.

She said, "Yes, I do feel different now. Not more important, but like I have more responsibilities, and I don't mind having the title ether."

"Wow," I said. "I'm asking because when I received my Black Belt in Kenpo I didn't feel any different. It was the same when I received my Practitioner License in Centers for Spiritual Living."

"It was the same for me with my Practitioners License," she said. "I felt the same before and after getting it. Receiving the license didn't change anything."

I knew this was different but I wondered what made it different. Was it that at the time of my Black Belt test and Practitioner License I already felt qualified? Was it was something more intangible; something that I just couldn't put my finger on?

"I guess it doesn't matter," I finally said to Nancy.

"You'll figure it out," she said with a smile.

"Let's get ready to go to Crater Lake," I said. "There's a nice little bed and breakfast waiting for us."

I had spoken to the chef of the restaurant at the B&B and let him know how we would need whatever Nancy ate to be pureed or softened so that she could swallow it. He assured me that they would accommodate her in any way they possibly could. I took him at his word. When we sat in the restaurant our order had been submitted before we arrived. I was having the salmon and Nancy would have the potatoes, well mashed, and a vegetable soup run through the blender or otherwise broken down to ease her condition. Towards the end of our meal they came through and asked us about breakfast. Nancy gave them some ideas and we were off. We still had a few hours of daylight and we didn't want to waste it. We went to the room to get unpacked and changed so we could sightsee.

The room was vintage 1920s except for the shower, which was equipped with all the good things: hand-held massage tools, good-smelling soaps, lotions, even a choice of shampoos and conditioners. Best of all for me, right outside the room was a plate of fresh baked cookies. Even though Nancy could not enjoy them she did enjoy smelling them. It was amazing. Even without the food it was an experience we could both savor.

The person at the front desk told us about the two waterfalls, one was located about a quarter of a mile down a dirt path and the second was located about a mile down the same path. We felt pretty fresh so we decided to go for it.

We arrived at the first waterfall very quickly and discovered it to be two separate waterfalls that flowed into a common pool. They were about twelve feet tall and there was a separation of about fifteen feet of land and trees between the two falls. The two falls formed a larger stream with lots of large trees that had fallen across the stream. The trees were so big we could have easily walked across to the other side of the stream if we choose to. Today, we decided to just stay on our side.

After taking in the amazing view we were still feeling pretty good so we decided to go the distance to the next bigger waterfall. This second waterfall was well over 100 feet tall, and we were told it was quite spectacular.

The second waterfall was not as good for us as the first. It was incredibly tall, but it fell through so many rocks that that it was hard to believe there was any water flowing through it. The rocks also seemed to muffle the sound of the water. We decided to head back to the inn, but along the way take lots of pictures, I knew my memory wouldn't be enough to remember all we had seen.

The next morning the chef had prepared a yogurt with fruit that Nancy said was incredible. He gave her a bowl that was at least as big as a dinner plate, and Nancy finished it all. I had not seen her be able to eat that much in several months. We asked for the chef to come out so we could compliment him. He came out and graciously accepted our praise, then to our surprise told Nancy there would be no charge. It was his pleasure to prepare it for her, and that whatever else she had that night and the next morning would be no charge as well. We felt completely blessed by the care and consideration we received from these people who didn't even know us.

With breakfast finished, we headed to Crater Lake. It was truly a sight to behold. The water was the deepest blue I have ever seen. The lake was formed entirely from snowmelt. There is no water inlet or outlet. It was formed in the crater made from a volcano many, many, years ago. Because of its remote location and elevation, the park is only open for four months out of the year.

We took the driving tour around the lake seeing it from all sides. We were taking pictures along the way and I found one shot that I just had to have. There was a light gray dead tree standing proudly alone on an outcropping that overlooked the lake on one of the very steep hillsides. At the base of the tree was a bundle of purple wild flowers that faced the lake. It was picturesque. I wanted the shot. It would involve me going to the edge of the crater. It was something I would never, ever consider doing, except that I had been using the Journey processes to get through my fears. This was a primary fear I had recently worked through.

I went to get the picture and as the shutter to the camera snapped I was pulled back in a very forceful way. It was Nancy. She was very concerned that I had leaned out too far. This is the lady that sat on the edge of the cliff. This is the lady that sat on the edge of the waterfall in northern Maine. This was the lady that had no fear, except one; that I might get hurt being careless.

It was a learning experience: Me discovering how fearless I had become, and her being both scared and excited to have her husband grow into someone who could now do almost anything for her.

Whenever I looked at Nancy, all I could see was strength and bravery. I knew she was vulnerable, and I knew she was in pain. I also knew I couldn't fix it, no matter how brave I was, but I still believed she could.

When we went down to breakfast the next morning we were delighted to see that Nancy's meal had once again been prepared and she said it was amazing. Our waitress, Ruth, after delivering our food went to talk to some of the children at the next table. She told them the hotel had some friendly ghost that liked to play tricks on the guests and asked if they had seen anything strange. They looked wide-eyed back at her and said, "Not yet."

At the same moment a drawer that was located behind Ruth opened seemingly by itself.

The self-opening drawer was located in a serving station that separated the kitchen from the dining room. The drawers actually went all the way through from the dining room to the kitchen, so the drawers could be filled on the kitchen side and then opened into the dining room to retrieve its contents. The people in the kitchen were pushing the drawers through from the back. It fooled the kids and their response entertained us throughout breakfast, as drawers opened seemingly at random.

These people who served us were masters. They took service to a level I had yet to experience in my life. They gave us exquisite memories that will last the rest of our lives. I pray that the knowledge of their contribution to us enriches their lives as much as it has enriched ours.

With our sights seen, and Nancy's achievements acknowledged, we prepared to go home and reengage with our world, which seemed to be too rapidly changing.

With each vacation we took our appreciation grew; not just for what we saw, but for the people we met. The sights were magnificent and majestic, but the way those we met were moved to do what they could to make our experience easier was in many ways more amazing, wonderful, and startling than any natural wonder. We saw kindness that has a tendency to be absent in everyday life. Or perhaps I had just missed it before. I wondered what the ladies at the retreat would have done if I had given them the same head's up that I gave the chef at the hotel. Lesson learned, I thought to myself.

Regardless, not a day went by that my heart was not opened at someone's act of generosity and kindness toward Nancy or even myself. We were both stepping into a life of gratitude that was deeper than either of us had experienced up to that point. I also knew the circumstance that helped create it.

Chapter 15

Tuesday, May 8, 2012, 11:00 a.m.

They are planning on doing a new tracheotomy on Thursday. They said after they do this you will be able to breathe even easier. They still have you sedated all the time but I am grateful that you are able to rest and get oxygen. You have been working so hard at breathing for so long. I'm hoping this will make a positive difference. I am very impressed with the care we have received while here.

I go to the house every day for cat feeding and some play time with them before cleaning the litter. This should be time for me to rest also but I just try to keep praying. It is easy to slip into fear. I stay here at the hospital except for the short visits home for the cats. Even though home is less than ten minutes away, and others are here to watch you, it's easier for me to be in that meditative place when I can see the healing taking place. For now, this is my new home.

FEEDING TUBE–2011

On the way back home we talked of the state fair and how going for her seemed silly. We go to eat fried food and there would be nothing for her to enjoy. She suggested I go with someone else. I suggested we start a new tradition of going somewhere else that we could both enjoy. There was light in her face at the thought of that. I believed at that time she was looking for a reason to live. I don't know.

The next evening before we went to sleep she said she had to come clean to me. She told me how the night before she had said she would be to bed in a few minutes and didn't come to bed for about an hour and a half. She said she had been in the Journey room crying. Sometimes she just wanted the pain to go away. No matter how that happened it didn't matter. It was like her spirit had finally been broken. At first I thought this is surrender and that is a step toward healing but I realized that it could have been resignation. The footing on which we stand is always shifting, always changing. I was not sure where she was.

I came clean also, I told her about my experience of wanting to experience death. I told her in detail what had happened at the retreat, and that to experience death I had to be the one to remain here. What we call dying was to be reborn. I also told her we are here to live life no matter what is going on around us. Grace does not care what experience we have. The most important thing is to stay open to the experience. We held each other for a long time that night, but like I said before, I knew it would never be long enough.

If we knew there was no death would we be more open to life? I don't know. It's hard to leave Nancy even for a minute. It seems I have a new greatest fear. It is not a fear of death, it is fear of separation.

It was getting very difficult for her to swallow even the mostly liquid diet we were following. Eating was very difficult for her, even at home where she could have a smoothie or protein shake. Her weight was dipping below ninety, but she was reluctant to commit to the abdominal feeding tube. I didn't understand why, because I knew with the tube she could get as much nourishment as she used to get by mouth. What I didn't know was how much it would really cost her when she finally agreed to the tube.

A little while after that night, we made an appointment with the gastroenterologist we'd been referred to. I'll call him Dr. Glendredge. We arrived at his office and discussed what life might be like with the tube. Nancy was seeing things as they were. She knew she could not continue to ingest the food she needed to survive without the tube. She needed this to survive. All I could see was her gaining weight, and regaining her energy through the use of this feeding tube and by doing so would gain the strength to heal herself. She could see she would never again enjoy any food by mouth. There was also another drawback to having the abdominal feeding tube. Nancy would no longer be able to swim, or bathe in the tub. The fact was for the most part everything she was losing she had already given up, but I believe there is a definite difference in having the choice of getting in the water and knowing you cannot get in the water without endangering your life.

It was decided that we should get the tube but it would be another two weeks before it could be done. Dr. Glendredge suggested that perhaps we might insert a breathing tube at the same time. Nancy gave a shake of the head that was the most emphatic, "NO," I had ever heard her say.

Nancy had been having trouble breathing also, and it was clear that the tumor was starting to obstruct her airway. Dr. Glendredge knew it. I could hear it in Nancy's speech and in her breathing. I could hear it at night and the sound of it sometimes kept me up. In time it would become something I could not sleep without hearing. When I asked her about it later she said she wanted to wait till the last minute to have the breathing tube put in. That statement, "The last minute" shook me to my core.

As the day for the operation approached one of Nancy's friends called about meeting us at the hospital. She was offering her support. Her name is Kerry, and she was in fact one of Nancy's oldest friends. She had followed Nancy's condition as all her friends had, but Kerry had the freedom to be able to arrange her day to be at the hospital with us.

There was a low time in her life when we visited Kerry and tried to support her as best we could. As I reflect, all of Nancy's close friends were like that. They took turns taking care of one another. If it wasn't one it would be someone else. I had friends like that also. I knew we would never need anything. We had a support team that would always be there for us. It was a comfort to us both.

We arrived early at the hospital the morning of the operation. There was no grand last meal for Nancy. There was no going out with a big anything. I went in with relief that she would be able to be nourished. Nancy went in with a sense of finality, and a lot of questions about how her life would be without something that had been a passion for her for most of her life. Each minute, each day that passed she could see how much more this affected not just her, but us. We would not be going out to eat anymore. We would not throw dinner parties with her friends. There would be no birthday cake. She would not have Christmas dinner or Thanksgiving. The celebrations of eating together would now be different. And as hard as others might try, Nancy would always be the one that would have our attention. They would feel guilty eating in front of her. She knew this. I knew this. Neither of us could think of anything that would change it, at least not right away.

Even though we were there early Kerry was waiting for us. We met up in one of the waiting rooms, until they were ready to begin. Dr. Glendredge told us that because Nancy's throat was affected by the tumor, they might not be able to get the tube in. The tube would be inserted into the stomach by pushing it down her throat and pulling it out through an incision in the abdomen. If they couldn't get the tube past her throat, they would have to do a major surgery where they would open the stomach.

I could see Nancy's tension growing as he spoke of this. I'm sure this was his job, but he certainly wasn't putting Nancy in a good place where she could be relaxed going in. When he was finished I asked for a minute with my wife. I assured Nancy that her body wanted to be nourished and it would relax for her and be open so that everything would go surprisingly well. This took a few minutes, as I had to convince myself as well. By the time they came in to sedate her we were both feeling a lot better.

A great teacher and man of science Albert Einstein stated it took four to eleven positives to overcome one negative comment. I was also aware of how our bodies held tension when we're stressed and how being relaxed made all our actions and reactions go much more smoothly. I understand the need for complete disclosure, but it is my belief that the need for compassion is greater, and our time together through our latest vacation had shown us that as well.

They sent me to the waiting area, where Kerry was already

seated. I sat down beside her and told her what they told me. I also told her about our prayer before they put her under that everything would go very well and she would be completely safe and that the surgery should only take about twenty minutes. Then we began our distraction talk where we try to keep each other's minds occupied so we won't be as worried.

Twelve minutes after we entered the room the nurse came in and said I could go and see Nancy in recovery. The procedure went flawlessly. I was led to Nancy's bedside and found her still sleeping. The doctor came by and said, "Mr. Carrier, the procedure went very well. As a matter of fact it was one of the easiest that I have ever done. Nancy did great and she should be waking up in a couple of minutes. As long as things look good after she wakes up you can get her home in about an hour."

"Thanks Doc," I said.

I then tended to Nancy. She was coming out of the anesthesia, looking at me with questioning eyes. I told her the procedure went very well and very fast, and that we would be able to go home soon.

I knew that Nancy would be concerned about what happened next, even though the feeding tube had been explained to us in detail. We had the food for the feeding tube and feeding syringes. We knew how to use it and how to clean it. I even had a special holder I made to hold the syringe so we could pour the food into it and just let gravity move the food to her stomach. This way her stomach received about the same amount over more time so it was more like eating at a normal pace. We also added a digestive enzyme to simulate the saliva mixing with the food before it entered her system.

Even with all these things we did ahead of time, there was still some apprehension. I tried to be assuring, but only going home and getting started would make things better. Kerry came in the room and she helped by reassuring Nancy that all was in place. Soon after, Kerry left and we went home to start a very different lifestyle.

We were told that Nancy could start using the tube right away, but we waited for several more hours before giving her the first meal with the tube. It went well and it gave her the feeling of being full for the first time in the last six months. It was something positive to hold onto at a time when there was little to be excited about.

As for me I was just happy she was home, safe, and able to live another day. Every day she was alive was another day there was a chance that she could turn this condition around.

We got calls, texts, and emails from all of Nancy's friends after Kerry had sent the message that she was okay. That was the medicine she needed. I could see her relax and feel a little better. She had made the only decision she could with the feeding tube. We would all support her. The question in my mind was how normal can I make this experience for her. What can we do to replace the time we would spend in restaurants with friends, and what about Nancy's trouble with being able to speak?

Kerry and Nancy worked out the last one. Kerry came by the next day to see how Nancy was doing. Nancy had been looking at Kerry's IPad and especially an app that enabled her to write on a fake yellow pad with her finger in place of a pencil or pen. It would allow Nancy to write without using paper. Nancy and I talked about it after Kerry left and we decided it might be a good thing to have. I told her I'd look into it in the morning.

Later that night I got a call from Kerry. She had some questions for me.

"Hi David, did you notice how much Nancy liked the tablet?"

"Yes I did. I was thinking about getting her one."

"I don't want to offend you in anyway David, but I was wondering if you'd let me pay for half? It would help me to feel better if I could do something to make a contribution, if you don't mind."

"Kerry it would please both me and Nancy if you wanted to do that. I would not feel at all insulted."

"Oh thank you David, you made my night. I'll go ahead and pick it up since I know what she wants and I can get the app she wants as well."

"That would be great Kerry, thanks for making things easy for me."

"Okay, I'll call you later."

We both hung up and I started to get things ready for bed, when my phone rang again. It was Kerry.

"Hi David, I called Lauren and Mary and they want to be in

on it too."

"Kerry, what are you really trying to say?"

"You don't have to pay anything at all, we have it covered."

"Well, as long as you asked," I said.

A few weeks later I found a Bluetooth keyboard to go with the IPad. I came home from a small job I was doing and asked Nancy if she would like one.

"Yes I think it would be faster for me to type and easier for people to read it," Nancy wrote.

Before I could say another word Nancy added, "Kerry picked one up and she's bringing it by later tonight."

Friends, they could do so much for us if only we gave them permission. I cannot count the times I dismissed offers from friends because of pride or just feeling unworthy. So many people that we knew and some we didn't know had shown us that to accept their gifts not only blessed us, but also enriched the life of the giver as well. Life was full of wins if only we could accept them. We didn't go to the fair that year. We changed our tradition from going to the fair, to being with friends.

Chapter 16

Wednesday, May 9, 2012, 7:00 a.m. This is your fourth day in the hospital.

You look so much better. The swelling is completely gone, there is almost no discernable additional mucus in the tank, even though we suction regularly. Yes, I have learned to do this as well. Your color is better too. I know you'll be awake soon. I want you to talk to me. I have a writing pad and pen ready. I want to know that I made the right decision. I know that wanting to know this is selfish, but I can't shake the guilt building inside.

PINK LADIES AND A NEW HAT–2011

Nancy had many friends, and while I would not intend to forget any of them, there were some that touched her heart in a unique way during the stressful time we were experiencing. They reminded her of times long past and gave her a feeling of always being connected, even when separated by miles, and years. For Nancy, one small circle of friends that were particularly close was the Hat of Hats Society. These were three friends she met in college.

They were three of many of her best friends. I'm not sure Nancy had any favorites as she loved them all for who they were and they were all very different. Some were about family, others about business, and some about the planet. They all loved each other beyond societal and religious boundaries. The one thing that bonded all of them together was the, "Hat of Hats." It looked like a sombrero on steroids, and it could have easily kept their shoulders dry in a driving rain. Nancy had a picture of each of them wearing this hat. It was always displayed in a place of honor.

I believe we all have friends we don't even know about, and some we will never forget. They always seem to show up at just the perfect time. It lets us know that we're connected beyond the things we can comprehend. It shows us our relationships with each other are more than business transactions, they're personal, and meaningful at the level of human spirit.

In 2011 our church put on a murder mystery party. Each of us would arrive at the party portraying a particular character. Nancy and I were disgruntled farmers. Others arrived as scientists, movie stars, writers, a botanist, and land owners. None of us knew who was going to die at the party, or who the murderer was. At one point during the party Nancy pointed to one of the many suspects and said, "I wonder if that woman over there will sell me her hat."

I must say I was taken aback. The hat was pink with a cap that fit closely to the head; on top of the cap were large pink rings encircling the dome. It looked like Saturn had changed color and was trying to escape the rings that orbited it. The rings came together at the center of the dome forming the outline of a clover. It was studded with white glass portrayed as diamonds, the largest of which was right in the middle. "You want to give someone money for that?" I asked.

"Go and ask if she'll sell it to me after the party," she asked.

I just looked at her. I knew she had a good reason for the request, but short of it being some long lost relic of the late Ms. Roosevelt, I figured she was one row short of a full crop. That of course did not stop me from asking the nice lady if she would be willing to sell me the hat.

She said she would gladly give it to me. This of course came as a relief as a hat of this caliber must be either trash or treasure. At least now I knew which it was. It was trash to the nice lady at the party, and it was treasure to the very nice and very happy lady that I would be going home with. She will be the one smiling wearing her new hat.

Except she didn't wear it, she tried it on once, and then set it down. She got on her email and started sending letters to her friends from the Hat of Hats Society. She told them she had the new Hat of Hats. A meeting was scheduled after that to determine the validity of the find. If in fact it was determined that this was the new Hat of Hats, then and only then would pictures be taken.

It took a few weeks to decide on the date, but all of the women showed up. It was an amazing day for Nancy. I actually believe that for a moment she forgot about what she couldn't do. Surrounded by her closest friends I believe she felt invincible. They talked for a long time as old friends do and I stayed well out of the way. It was so good just watching all of them smile, but the biggest smile was on Nancy. She could still host a gathering, and do it well. It was a proud day for her.

Eventually, I was invited into the room and took pictures of each one wearing the new hat of hats. Later I would give each of them two pictures; one of themselves, and one of Nancy, each wearing the Hat of Hats.

Later in the week one of Nancy's lifelong friends was also invited to have her picture taken with the hat, and for the first time in close to forty years, the Society had a new member. For Nancy I would matte and frame all of them wearing the Hat of Hats. In hung in our home in a place of honor, so she could always be reminded of the day.

Things were changing at our house. It seemed we would each be wearing slightly different hats. The mealtime was similar to what it was before, but with the feeding tube there were other considerations. Now we also had some special meal in a bottle that had lots of nutrients and calories that could help her gain back some weight. I could drink the smoothies but the liquid meals they gave us were not made to be tasted. This was minor compared to the challenges we found in the bathroom.

We had two bathrooms in the house, one that had a traditional tub-shower combination, and one that had a separate shower and tub, which was the master bath. She was okay in the shower but she still worried about getting water where the tube went into her stomach. I installed a hand-held showerhead that she could direct the water as she wished and then we added a shower seat, to make it even easier. I also installed a lower shampoo and soap holder that hung down below the shower valve. Everything was in arms reach when she was seated and soon she felt confident bathing in our new shower setup.

In no time at all she had gained back about six pounds. I could still see her ribs but they were much less pronounced. She also had more energy. Except for the changes I mentioned she was getting back to her old self. I was pleased with her progress. Our house was now set up for her to be able to do everything she needed to do. It gave her some independence. This was something she needed. I needed to remember to let her do things for herself, and I needed to remember to do things for myself as well. We were a team, but we both needed to feel we were pulling our own weight.

It was during these times that we really began to focus on anything we could find to feel better. We looked at all of Nancy's friends and the Hat of Hats Society. We took our photo albums of our wedding and the big vacations we had taken. We started counting all of the good things we had experienced together and decided we were not finished. It was time to start something new.

We put our heads together as we often did. We would place the centers of our foreheads close and then gently move in closer till they touched. We would look closely into each other's eyes then close our eyes and open our hearts and minds to thoughts of adventure. This exercise was always easy for me, and Nancy was a master. Most of the trips we took were her idea. I would ask her things like "How can you die first, when you're the one who knows how to live?"

"Who says I'm dying first," was her usual reply. This time however, things were different. We were forgetting that there were things we still wanted to do. Darkness was moving in. Dreams were scarce and we were having a hard time seeing any light shining through the cracks of our reality. We needed to find a way to swim to the surface of sorrow into the light of new life, and new positive experiences before we drowned. At the edge of every cliff Nancy always chose life, but right now she was having trouble deciding, and without her, I was having trouble deciding too.

I believe in order to go where you want to go, before you can plan the journey or even take the first step you have to know where you want to go, or have an intention as to what you want to achieve. I knew what I wanted. I wanted Nancy to change the direction of her health failing to her getting better. My view of our situation was that the feeding tube was a good thing because she could once again nourish her body, gain back some weight, feel healthier in some way, and use this as a stepping stone to clear her thinking and her belief system around her ability to heal herself. For her it was different.

Nancy saw this as the next step of surrendering to the cancer. The ability to eat was the next thing that had been taken away. I did not suspect at the time but I am sure she was thinking about what might be taken away next.

When she lost her voice I realized that an important part of our ability to communicate had been lost too. She talked much more than she wrote. Without the inflexions in her voice, I lost much of the meanings of what she was telling me. As I said before, being foolish comes easy to a man. I always believed she could and would do whatever was necessary to heal herself through sheer will. At the time of this writing the phrase that comes to me is, we see things as we are, not as they are... It never occurred to me she might be giving up.

Chapter 17

Wednesday, May 9, 2012, 11:30 a.m.

We are waking you up today before they do the surgery tomorrow. I am grateful, as we can assess your condition more thoroughly. As you come out of the anesthesia you ask for a writing pad but when I give you the pad and pen you are too groggy to write. I try to take them back but you will not release the pen. You have super-human strength on the grip of your means of communication. When you can write, you tell me about the Blue Star Angel who visited you. I am feeling good about making the right decisions when you write, "I want to return to my Heavenly Home."

Upon reading this my heart breaks and I wonder if this is what you really want or if it is the drugs. To save my sanity I decide to give you more time to gain consciousness. You've been kept pretty groggy because they want to keep you on the ventilator, but they also want to communicate with you so they can assess your condition. The more you wake up the more you seem like your old self. Everyone is so pleased that you have returned to us that we have a small celebration and prepare for tomorrow's surgery. But the celebration does nothing to quiet the voice of doubt about my decision to try to keep you alive.

WAKING UP–2012

It's Thursday morning, the fifth day in ICU, the condition that had been a small distraction at the beginning of each chapter of this book and our lives, has finally taken center stage. No longer will there be two stories; one about cancer, one about living. From now on it's about living with cancer.

This is the point where our stories come together; where our fears around cancer meet, and test our faith in recovery. We will no longer act as if the special diet was just to be healthy. We will no longer forget there was a feeding tube between meals because it wasn't visible beneath her clothes. Her condition was now in full view for all to see.

Everyone who supported us and worked so hard to believe in our miracle would go from faith to fear, even if just for a moment. The breathing tube would be visible. It would need to be suctioned often throughout the course of the day. It would remind us that her health was deteriorating. Unless we received the miracle we did our best to expect, it was time to let everyone we knew see what was happening.

My biggest concern before we came to the hospital was that Nancy had given up. Then her heart stopped. Then she came back. Then she told me she wanted to return to her Heavenly Home. Now I don't know what to believe. I want to support her. I don't know how.

We were up most of the night with the normal routine that Nancy used to sleep through. She still isn't fully conscious but I tell her everything that has happened the last few days. I let her know how successful she was at waiting till the last minute.

In the morning they explain to me that all surgery has risk but they feel very confident in her abilities to pull through with ease and grace. I have to admit that I am not at all nervous about it. There is a deep knowing that she will be all right. After they take Nancy out of the room I head to the cafeteria for some food. Before I can get back they've finished and Nancy's safe in ICU. The talk is that after a few days we'll be moved to a regular bed in the main hospital, then go home as soon as the social worker sets things up for us. I am so ready for this to be over. I know Nancy will feel better at home.

True to their word, two days after the surgery we're in a regular room. The funny thing is for most being in the hospital is a serious thing, but after so many days in ICU it's like being home already. We have more time to ourselves and the biggest concern is now getting to the bathroom and bathing, as opposed to just living through the next few hours. Just two days later we're in the car and heading home.

Home sweet home was all I could feel, as I walked into our house. We walked to the couch and sat down. I asked about the TV but Nancy shook her head no, so I asked about some music and got a yes. She wrote down what CD to play and I put it on. As the music started to play I began to get her smoothie ready, Nancy motioned for me to come over. I knelt down in front of her and in her best voice, her only voice, as painful as it was, pushed air up around the breathing tube, through her vocal cords and said. "I Love You."

I can only imagine how much effort it took for her to do that. I knew it had to be very painful. Hearing it certainly brought me to tears. I held her for a long time after that. It's the one thing in this lifetime I can honestly say I will always, always remember. I feared it would be the last thing I would ever hear her speak.

TUESDAY MAY 26, 2012: THE TIME IS NOW.

In total, Nancy spent seven days in ICU, and two more days in a regular hospital room remembering how to walk and being taught how to bathe without getting water near the breathing tube. Nancy mastered her new skills very quickly and we got to go home nine days from the morning we first arrived. I didn't ask her about the Blue Star Angel or her returning to her Heavenly Home. I didn't want to hear the answer.

Chapter 18

SMELLING THE FLOWERS–MAY 2013

In the last year my dear Nancy lost the ability to eat. She got the feeding tube. Never again would any food pass her lips. Never again would she taste anything that once brought her pleasure.

She lost the ability to breathe through her nose and mouth. This meant she needed a tracheotomy. She had to have a suction machine with her at all times to keep the inner cannula in the breathing tube clear of mucus.

She lost the ability to speak. This meant she had to carry a pen and paper with her to communicate with others.

With the pain medication she couldn't drive a car because it made her so sleepy.

When she lost the ability to swallow, it meant carrying around an emesis basin so she could release her saliva. The average person makes over a quart of saliva a day. Because the tumor obstructed her throat, the saliva could not go to her stomach. Because she could not move her tongue, she could not spit it out. She would have to lean her head forward every now and then and let it drain out.

When she slept she positioned her head so that the saliva would drain into the basin. I placed a folded paper towel in the bottom of the basin, to keep the saliva from spilling if the basin got tipped. This embarrassed her when she went out so I suggested she use a travel mug. This way she could look like she was taking a sip, when she was actually draining her mouth of excess saliva.

It gets to be easier and easier to be isolated when the ability to lead what we call a normal life ends. It is amazing how much we have to lose that we take for granted each day. It's easy for me to be discouraged or angry when things don't go my way.

If I don't like my food I send it back or just order something else. If I want something I ask for it. If I'm happy I sing or laugh, if I'm sad enough I cry. I never really realized how much these seemingly little things made my life so wonderful, but things change. Now I wonder if I didn't have them, could I still be grateful for what is left.

The last thing to go up to this point was her sense of smell. With no air going through her nasal passages there was no way for her to smell anything. I believed there was nothing left to lose. I thought there was nothing left to torment her for the time she had left. I was wrong.

She had experienced mouth pain after the tracheotomy and discovered a tumor at the front of her mouth. It was pushing on her front teeth. At the beginning of 2013 its growth accelerated and began pushing her lower front teeth up and out. Because she could not move her jaw the dislodged teeth were cutting into the roof of her mouth, causing severe pain. As the tumor became more pronounced she became disfigured. The tumor became so large she could not close her lips together. I never ever thought of Nancy as anyone other than the beautiful being I knew she was, and when I was with her at that time I never noticed any different behavior from those around us. I believed they couldn't help but see her as I did.

Nancy was always very concerned about how she looked and I never thought about how she might feel going into public with this new condition. I'd like to think my seeing Nancy the way I did must have helped, because she never covered her face at all during the last several months, even when we left the house. She still put on good clothes and took care of her appearance. Looking back, I am pleased by this. Perhaps she saw herself as I saw her.

I often wondered how much one could endure before finally giving up. This was enough for Nancy. Nancy and I planned a trip to the lake house in May of 2013. This would be our last trip. On this trip I did all the packing. I prepared her food, clothes, cleaning kits for her trach, the suction machine, and anything else I could think of. I wanted to do everything I could to make every moment she had as pleasant as possible.

I noticed that over the last month that being in the car made Nancy more nauseous, so I always tried to keep a steady speed, and make any turns or changes in direction smooth and easy. On this trip to the lake that proved to be impossible. It was a two-hour drive in normal traffic, but then there was an accident in the city of Temple. As a result, we were stop and go for over thirty miles. This added over forty minutes to the drive and made the trip torturous to Nancy. When we finally arrived I got the house prepared, and I had her lay down for a brief nap to recuperate.

I felt helpless that day. There are no tortures that I can imagine that could have been worse than what this beautiful woman endured the last four months and she still had more life to live. With every wince and every tear she shed, I felt the fire of the words I had said in the ER one year before. "Do what you can to keep her alive."

As I looked at her lying on the bed, finally getting some small moment of relief, I felt the full weight of my selfishness. Had I known this is what I was asking of her, I am sure, as painful as it would have been that I would have let her go. Now more than ever, my life belonged to her. I owed her every ounce of effort I had in me to do anything I could to give her relief.

Once she was resting as comfortably as possible, I quietly cleaned up and set up the things we would be using on our visit. I knew that it would be a while before the nausea would subside so she could eat, so I set aside the food, and started preparing the basins with the paper towels. I liked to have about five of these ready ahead of time, and we had used three on the way here. After this I laid down beside Nancy to rest.

I couldn't help but wonder what this place would be like without her. She loved this cabin. It was a place where she found rest; a place where her demons couldn't find her. She would go outside and look at the lake for hours, and just sit and read. Most of the time there was little or no boat traffic, so all that could be heard was the sounds of nature. For her, it was a place to be grounded, where she would not be swept into the vortex of day-to-day worries that were so intrusive in her consciousness. This was her place of peace, and even if cancer followed her here, it didn't have the same power as when we were home. This was something to be grateful for. The horrid drive was now behind us, it was time for rest.

When Nancy awoke I sat up next to her on the bed. Wordlessly we gazed into each other's eyes, and slowly leaned in until our foreheads touched. We then closed our eyes, holding hands and taking in the deep connection we had forged together. These were the moments that made all time fade away, where our hearts became one, and we knew only the love we shared. We stayed this way until we were sure the moment was etched into all eternity, and then pulled away smiling at each other, all the while knowing it was these times that would sustain us when everything else was gone.

I asked Nancy if she could take some food and she nodded, yes. I set up her meal and then prepared something for myself. We stayed together while we ate and for the first time since we had been going there together, we spent the rest of the evening being quiet together. We usually watched a rented movie or one that I had brought from our Grand Prairie home. This time was different. This was why we came to the lake house; to be alone, and to be together. As for the rest of the weekend, we would spend it taking short walks, sitting in the backyard by the water, and watching the wild deer that liked to hang out in the front yard each morning and evening. It was a pleasant time and we soon forgot about all the things we couldn't do, and remembered all we could do.

We could still hold hands, and feel the connection that was our first point of contact with each other. The same hands that offered comfort and loving caresses the last seven years we had been together. We could still look into each other's eyes, and see into each other's souls without blocks or boundaries. We could still place our right hands on each other's hearts and feel the one heartbeat that sustained us, and let us know that we were inseparable. We could look at each other's faces, and communicate with a glance what mere words could not convey.

We could still embrace and feel the warmth of each other's bodies, each supporting the other in a way that neither of us could do alone.

It was in this way that Nancy let me know that there were things we had lost, but the things that were most important, we still had. And we would find a way to keep those things alive in us, because our love was not bound by time or space.

When the last day came I went to talk to our closest neighbor, to tell him we wouldn't be out for a while. As I walked around the cabin to a break in the fence between our houses I looked down and realized I almost stepped on a baby deer. It was about the size of a puppy, and it was lying perfectly still in some ground cover that was alongside the house. I slowly backed up and went up to the roof to take a picture of it from above. I went inside and showed Nancy the picture. She followed me outside and it was still there, but while I was inside it had reoriented itself.

We looked around and saw what we believed to be the mother on the other side of the wooden fence that separated the properties. It was then we realized she would be back soon to take care of her fawn. We went back into the house so they would not be disturbed.

In all Nancy's years enjoying this place she had never seen a newborn fawn. To us it was a fulfillment of the promise that life goes on, and it was as close as our own side yard. We both felt blessed; for our love and closeness and for all that had been shown to us.

It wasn't about choosing life any more; life goes on. It was about choosing to notice the beauty all around us. Tomorrow we may be someplace else, and when we are will we be marveling at the beauty that is there or missing what we no longer have?

I told Nancy, "Every moment we have is precious, so let's never again waste our time sitting on a highway moving at two miles per hour, when we can get off the highway and see something, or just stop the car and talk to one another, until things get moving. One of the few things we cannot control is the movement of time. I promise not to waste any more of it than I already have."

Chapter 19

THE RIGHT THING TO DO–JULY 2013

The nausea began with the feeding tube but was off and on at first, now it was almost constant. I remembered when her sodium was low this was one of the signs, and I got a little concerned. Whenever I called her GP I was told to just go to the emergency room so I didn't think twice about it. They took us in right away, and got our blood work taken. The doctor prescribed an IV that would stop the nausea right away, and it worked wonders. Nancy felt immediate relief. It was a little cold in the room and Nancy asked for a blanket. The nurse happily took one out of the cupboard and began to place it on her when she suddenly stopped. She looked intently at Nancy and asked, "Were you in here about a year ago?"

Nancy shook her head yes.

The nurse said, "I just knew it was you. We worked on you a long time." She paused, "Did we do the right thing?"

I had thought about this almost every day for the last year. The real question was; did *I* do the right thing. I had never asked this, even though I desperately wanted to know. I looked at Nancy and asked, "Would you like me to wait outside?"

Nancy took my hand and shook her head "No." Nancy then looked at the nurse, with compassion and grace and nodded her head "Yes. You did the right thing."

The nurse then asked, "Was it worth it?"

Nancy took her pad and wrote, "Yes it was. It's been a good year, I'm glad I didn't miss it."

There were tears in the nurse's eyes as she held Nancy's gaze. No words were said, but she came over and squeezed Nancy's hand then left.

It was then I looked into Nancy's eyes and asked her. "Years ago for my birthday you asked me what I wanted most, and I said, 'More time.' Was this the fulfillment of my request?"

Nancy smiled and nodded, "Yes," then wrote, "I love you."

I knew that her love for me was greater than anything I had ever known. She gave me the essence of what true love really is. It's not giving your life over to death. It's giving your life over to those that need you most, no matter what the cost. In that moment she taught me how to fully love someone. Others might say that I gave that love to Nancy the whole time we were together. I knew I gave without resentment, or any reservation. I never held anything back from her, but now I realized she gave me even more. With her, I knew unconditional love. For the rest of her life, I never felt tired. I was always ready to serve her needs no matter what, without hesitation. She taught me how to be the one thing I always wanted to be; A Superhero.

Chapter 20

NOBODY'S HOME–JULY 2013

It's amazing how difficult it can be to connect with doctors. The gastrointestinal surgeon's office will not return my calls. I had called many times and asked about an extension to add to the feeding tube in Nancy's abdomen. I had tried to order one online and could not find one that I could be sure would work. They had given me an extension for the tube in the past and I was trying to get another. I'm wondering just what it was that was keeping them from a simple call.

After three weeks of desperation I decide to call Nancy's primary care doctor to see if he could get in touch with the other doctor and get me some answers. Two weeks and six calls later neither doctor's office had called back. Desperate times call for desperate measures, and I was desperate. I drove to her primary care doctor's office. I walked in and asked to see someone about un-returned phone calls for the last two weeks. A charge nurse asked me to come around to the side and took my information. A few minutes later she came back. She said, "The doctor has talked to the specialist, and at this point there is nothing more we can do. We recommend hospice care. If you'd like we can recommend several organizations."

I wanted to ask them if they were just hoping she'd die so they never had to call me back. I wanted to let them know that every patient they have has fear of dying and if you're going to wash your hands of a patient, it's appropriate to say goodbye, not just ignore them like someone you want to break up with but don't want to hear the tears. I wanted to tell them that the worst damage you can do to someone you have a relationship with is ignore them. I wanted to say all those things, but instead I just said, "I'll get back to you." It was as mean as I could be. Then I thought about Nancy.

I realized that all the competent authorities that she knew in conventional medicine were now jumping off a sinking ship. The only ones left were those who considered all of a lifetime to be sacred; not just the part that they get to participate in. Those were the doctors and practitioners on her holistic team. I was now the messenger. I had been given the news and now it was up to me relay the message first to Nancy, and then to her team. I felt like I was the sinking ship, and all the rats that had been running the show were jumping off because they had seen too many ships go down to watch another. Perhaps it made them think of their own mortality. It only made me wonder how she would feel when I told her.

I drove home wondering what to do. The shoe was on the other foot. I was now the one responsible for delivering the news, and I had no experience. I had read about doctors giving the news in books and watched it in movies. "I'm sorry Mr. Smith, there's not much more we can do." Or, "It's time to get your affairs in order." I wanted Nancy to feel supported, not abandoned. Even though that's the way I felt. I needed to choose my words carefully and I needed to set my intention to her comfort as opposed to my anger.

"Nancy, I talked to the doctors, and they said they're at the end of their rope. They feel like the only thing left for them to do is recommend hospice care. How do you feel about that?" I said.

It wasn't much but it was honest and to the point. Nancy nodded her head and to my surprise looked relieved.

It was like she had been given permission to stop fighting. For the first time I thought that maybe it was right for the doctors to give the news to me. It wasn't that Nancy needed to hear it. It was that I needed to hear it. It was like everyone was trying to get me to let go, like I was the only one who couldn't see the truth. For the first time since I first saw my beloved Nancy,

I realized that she was ready to go and my heart was breaking. She left the decision up to me at the time her heart stopped in the ER. I wanted more time and she gave it to me. She needed me to let go. Hospice could give her the one thing no one else seemed to be able to–relief from most of the pain. She wasn't coming back this time, and she was telling me that from the time she first gained enough consciousness to be able to write, after her heart stopped a year ago, "I want to return to my Heavenly Home." She had given me another year, now it was my turn to give her the dignified end that she deserved, and be fully present to her final wishes.

I spoke with Beth, one of Nancy's oldest friends, and she recommended a holistic hospice group. I called them to set up an appointment. I left a message and they returned my call within the hour. It was a refreshing change from what I had grown accustomed too.

I met with Dan, the founder, the next day and after a lengthy discussion decided to have them come in about an hour a day Monday through Friday. They let me know that when I was ready they could provide 24-hour care on very short notice. I was able to stay home with Nancy so there was no need for more than that at the time. I think they may have believed I was overestimating my abilities as she was getting a dose of morphine every ninety minutes around the clock, and it was difficult for her to self-medicate. I assured them that when I was ready I would call them immediately.

Dan was indeed a blessing, as he acquiesced to my request without argument and reminded me to call when the time came they could go to 24-hour care within an hour of notification. They were a blessing not because of what they did, but because of what they allowed me to do. They gave me the time to be Nancy's primary caregiver, and support us both in a way that allowed us to be with each other during the most intimate time of our shared lives.

In the past, when my first wife left me, I felt like I lost everything. I just wanted to hold onto something. I grasped for anything I could call mine that no one could take away. At that time, for me it was the house we lived in. It was silly really. I didn't even want it, yet it was the one thing that let me know I had some sort of value. This time it would be the memories we shared. They were mine to keep and no one could take them from me. What I didn't know was how meaningful and rich the rest of our time would be.

Nancy was hanging on as best she could. The one thing she had left that she wanted to be able to do was to get to the bathroom. She didn't mind me helping her, but it was one thing she could do with dignity. She didn't want anyone else cleaning her bottom. Being able to go to the bathroom gave her a sense of freedom. I could see it in her. I knew when the day came that she could no longer go in the bathroom, even with my help, it would mark her end. I'm not sure how I knew this, with any level of certainty. Some things we just know.

Our hospice experience started with a visit from the nurse, followed by a delivery from the pharmacy. Nancy got an oral shot of morphine. I was administering it with a small syringe (no needle) into her mouth between her cheek and gum. It was quickly absorbed into her bloodstream and she found relief very quickly. She also got a new patch for nausea. Both worked better than anything she had been on thus far. The nausea was gone in about thirty minutes, and her pain level dropped to almost pain free, in a matter of minutes. It was the best she had felt in about two years. And seeing her comfortable did wonders for me as well.

Having hospice in place I believed should have created a sense of finality, yet it felt more like a beginning. It gave me a sense of having more time, even though time was running out. Before, all I could see was the suffering going on and on. Now the pain would be eased. I saw the relief in Nancy when I asked her about bringing in hospice and now I was feeling it too.

At first, Nancy was getting her morphine at ninety-minute intervals. The nurse warned us to stay ahead of the pain. If her pain were allowed to get too high, it could take a lot more time to get it under control. We only slipped up one time and her pain level went up to almost unbearable. We had to increase the dose to bring it back down and it took almost thirty minutes. After that if there was any increase in pain we upped the dose by a small amount. We were told we could go as quickly as every thirty minutes between doses and we could increase the dosage by as much as three times what we were giving her now.

She gave us several extra syringes and I filled them all keeping them in a sterile cup until needed. At night I would set the countdown timer on my phone for ninety minutes and have it wake me so I could administer the morphine throughout the night.

After the first night I set up for visitors to come and see her. The list that Nancy made for who was allowed to come was short: Her oldest sister, several of her closest friends, her brother, and our minister. I arranged the times according to their convenience, so they would not all be there on the same day. I also let them know before they went in to see her that the tumor in the front of Nancy's mouth had grown quite a bit larger. All this was done under Nancy's guidance and with her approval. I told her she could change her mind at any time and I would send people away. It was only about what Nancy wanted.

I never lost faith that she could heal. I believed she could just stand up and walk out of the room laughing, and saying, "Well that was fun, what do you want to do next?"

For now, it was just about keeping up with her medication and feeding her twice a day; enough to give her nutrition, but not enough to aggravate the nausea. She still spent a few hours a day on the couch in the living room watching some TV and in some ways things seemed like they were getting back to normal. Of course this wasn't true. We were really just finding a place of calm acceptance of what seemed inevitable. Nancy felt better than she had in a long time, but the fact was that she was dying. It was a fact that was coming at me like a freight train. I, however, was just standing at the mouth of the tunnel looking at the simple light that was moving closer and closer to me, wondering what might be behind it. I guess as I said earlier in the story, I was still in the rowboat going after Moby Dick. Looking back, I would never change my belief that a miracle could happen to us. We already had so many miracles, I had faith there could be one more.

It was easy to see that Nancy was in a place of calm acceptance. Back in the ICU after she woke up, one of the first things she wrote was, "I want to return to my Heavenly Home." I was choosing to believe in the possibility of her choosing to stay, but the reality was she was ready to go. Like so many journeys we had gone on in our time together she was all packed and knew exactly what she wanted to take with her.

She never shared this, but I believe she found peace in her acceptance. Her only regret, was leaving me, and finding a way to make that okay would be my challenge, although I didn't know it at the time.

Chapter 21

SEPTEMBER 2013–THE END

After about three weeks on hospice Nancy had increased her morphine dosage by about ten percent and had increased the frequency to every hour and fifteen minutes. She was staying in the bedroom the whole day now and I was switching off with our hospice worker Martha, on bathing duties.

When it came to washing Nancy's hair she didn't like the no rinse product that was usually used, she really wanted to be shampooed. In her weakened condition we could not have her in the tub or the shower. This meant we needed some creativity to get the job done. Nancy usually sat in a chair to bathe, and the care worker would wash her using several buckets of water; one clean and one soapy. Nancy preferred this because the wipes left her skin dry and itchy.

With this in mind I found a way to wash Nancy's hair with her seated in the chair. I made a contraption that collected the water and funneled it into a trash can. All she needed to do was lean forward with her head toward her knees. The tray I made was three sided so the water that wet her head would flow out the end that was open, and flow into a waiting trash can that had been placed between her legs. In this way we were able to actually wash her hair with the shampoo she liked and have her hair dried and fixed the way she liked. It was something small, but it was something that was close to normal, and one of the few things that could make her feel like she looked the way she used to. With bathing done, there was still a lot of time left to do other things.

We filled our days with me reading to her and in the evening we watched movies. I installed a service where we could watch TV shows on the tablet and the computer, but Nancy had no interest in the shows she used to watch. It was enough that I was reading to her, talking to her, and holding her hand. She paid little attention to the movies in the evening but we laid together and held hands and watched.

This was as close as we had ever felt to each other. We just got lost in each other's gaze for hours. Then one day she looked at me, with some concern on her face.

I had completed my studies for the Beloved Community seminary program and was scheduled to be ordained in Oregon in early August. I did this right before Nancy started to need more care. As a result of her condition I withdrew from the ceremony and signed up for the next one, which was in October. It was now September.

Nancy wrote, "Your Ordination is next month. What if I'm still here?"

"I'll be right here beside you," I said. "My ordination is not a concern. I'm not going to start a church right now. And besides, you can't go right now. I'll be ordained when it's time. For now I just want to be with you. It's the most important thing in the world to me."

Nancy nodded her head to say, "Okay."

Later that day my phone rang. It was my mentor from the Beloved Community. They had discussed the situation and said if I needed to be with Nancy through the time where I would have been ordained, that they would send a team to Texas to perform the ceremony at my house. It was amazing the level of commitment the organization had to each of us.

I ran into the bedroom so she could hear what was being said. She just laid her head on my shoulder. I said to her, "These things have a way of working themselves out."

We didn't need a movie that night. We just lay beside each other knowing that no matter what our situation was, we were being blessed beyond measure. We took each moment that night and stretched it into a year. It was like a lifetime in one night, and I had never felt so much love. My phone alarm woke me from the trance. It was time for a morphine shot, and to change the patch that was now controlling her nausea.

A few days later Nancy told me she was done eating. The nausea had returned despite the medication to keep it down and the reduction in food intake. She weighed less than 60 lbs. at the time. Our time would be down to days.

THREE DAYS LEFT

Nancy had been doing pretty well with going to the bathroom with my help. This came as a surprise to those who had seen her recently. They couldn't believe she could come close to supporting her own weight. I would have been surprised as well had I not known her. Her body may have been weak but her resolve was amazingly strong.

When a trip to the bathroom was necessary it always began with Nancy sitting up. Then we would wait for the fluid to drain from her nose and mouth. Nancy would lower her head forward and then we would wait. This usually took about five minutes. She would then move her legs to drape over the side of the bed, and when she was ready, we would go slow moving steadily to the commode. It had a padded seat that brought some comfort, but not enough. It would take a few minutes to get there but it was all okay. This is something I am very grateful for. I have read horror stories of cancer patients at this stage of their death being in excruciating pain because of blockages, or constipation. I'm grateful for Nancy that with everything else that is going on she at least can go to the bathroom.

I have noticed that as time has gone on both Nancy and I have gone from missing the things we could do, to appreciating everything we can still do. We know that such simple things as brushing your teeth can be lost and what remains is generally less pleasant. The thought of what these last days may bring could have me paralyzed in fear; but instead I reside in gratitude for each moment, for each simple pleasure, and for each time we look into each other's eyes. I know once gone, they will be gone for the rest of my time here on earth.

I finished the book I was reading to Nancy, tonight. She does not want me to start another one. I'm not sure if it's because it's getting harder for her to concentrate, or because she feels she will not hear the end of it. It doesn't matter. The TV is mostly off and I'm happy with just being with her.

TWO DAYS LEFT

It's her second day without food or water. I see little change in her. With her spirit I would have a hard time believing she could be anything less than fully conscious.

She wrote me a note today. Just two words, "I'm Sorry." After I read them I looked at her face. Those two simple words were saying much more than could be understood by just reading them. "I'm Sorry."

She was saying "I'm sorry for being sick; for being in bed where you have to take care of me. I'm sorry for all you must do just to keep me alive for a few more days. I'm sorry for the money it cost us. I'm sorry for leaving you all by yourself. I'm sorry for the time I have taken away from your life where you have had to be here instead of doing something pleasant. I'm sorry we haven't been able to go out to eat for almost two years. I'm sorry I can't make love to you or even kiss you. I'm sorry I look like this. I'm sorry I can't make myself better for you... I'm Sorry."

I have been told and I have believed there are no words that can be spoken to make anyone feel better who is in a position like this. But I believe in God, and I believe in Nancy and I believe all things are possible.

I can't say where the words came from, but I knew what to say, and for the first time I was truly glad to be totally and completely selfish.

I looked at my sweet beloved and held her gaze for a moment. I smiled at her and said, "I hope you don't think that all I've done for you is free. If that's what you believe you've got another thing coming. Know this my love. I will take care of you for as long as I have breath in me. You can count on me. I will always be here for you. BUT, when you leave this earthly place and go to the other side of the veil, PLEASE, please, please remember, it's your turn to take care of me. Because that's when I'm really going to need you."

As the words and tears left my face I could see her face soften, and her eyes crinkled into a smile. Her body relaxed and I knew that through some miracle she was empowered. She had something to do, and something to look forward to. She knew I believed in her continuing on, and that I still wanted to be part of her when I was the one who couldn't hear her words or touch her skin, or see her smile.

She picked up her pad and wrote. "I love you."

I smiled.

She wrote again, this time larger: "I LOVE YOU."

This was so she could make sure I heard it.

THE LAST DAY

It is three a.m. and Nancy has awakened and needs to go to the bathroom... NOW. I quickly rise and help her out of bed. Blood and mucus flows freely over her clothes and the sheets. She only gets a few steps and starts to fall. I catch her and get her back to bed. She's disoriented and semi-conscious. I placed one of the absorbent pads beneath her and ask her to just pee in the bed. I assure her it will be okay and I'll clean everything up.

I will need to change the sheets. There is blood, mucus, and saliva everywhere. I doubt she would have been able to sit up for the five to ten minutes it takes to drain. It's okay, I tell myself, I've done this before with Nancy in the bed.

After she had voided her bladder, I cleaned up the pad, then as gently as I could I replaced her pillowcases and the sheets on the bed. I also changed her shirt and panties. She seemed to be resting well after that. I went on with her morphine every hour and got a little rest.

About five a.m. she woke up again insisting to go to the bathroom. I told her I had a pad in place and had placed the disposable pad under her so she could go in bed. She started to get up on her own. I came around to her side of the bed and reasoned that the last time we tried this she passed out. She looked at me and said with her eyes, "Are you going to help me or should I head to the commode on my own?"

I moved her arm around my head for support and began walking with her. She made it to the potty and rather than trying to take her panties off I told her to just pee through them, and I would clean her up. This time she complied with my wishes. When she finished I walked her back to bed and cleaned her up as promised.

When I was finished I asked her if it was okay for me to put the disposable panties on her, because it was getting difficult for her to walk and I was afraid she might get hurt.

This time she nodded, “Yes.”

I put the panties on her. I knew she would not get up again.

Since she was awake; I let her know that I thought it was time to call hospice, and tell them I needed round-the-clock help. I assured her that I would be here to do everything I had been doing and that I would be right here in the room. I would only leave her side to retrieve food or go to the bathroom. She agreed that it was time. I told her I wouldn’t call until about nine or ten that morning, and she let me know that was okay too. I kissed her good night and she closed her eyes. She would not open them again. I stayed up after that making sure she got her morphine, and keeping an eye on her. Her breathing was regular as always. She looked at peace, but I didn’t sleep.

I had called hospice as planned and they arrived shortly after ten to get everything set up. At that point I knew Nancy was probably in a coma, as she was totally unresponsive. That didn’t keep us from talking to her. We continued to communicate what was going on and who was there.

Later that day our friend Kim arrived at about 4:30 in the afternoon. I let her know what was going on, and took her back to be with Nancy. They had always shared a strong bond of friendship, and I knew Nancy would be okay with her there. Kim sat on the bed next to her and talked to her as she stroked Nancy’s hair. We stayed together for a while then I left Kim with Nancy to meet with Steve our hospice nurse.

I had always known that Nancy would not leave while I was in the room. We had discussed this during our time together over the last five weeks; she said it would be too difficult. I had known it since the final Journey retreat. When Steve and I came back into the room about ten minutes later, Kim was still stroking

Nancy's hair. Steve and I both looked at Nancy. She was gone.

Kim later told me that she had seen her and Nancy walking on the beach together while their eyes were closed, and she was stroking Nancy's hair. She said that before we came in, in her dream Nancy had asked what time it was. Kim told her it was 5:56. We entered the room at 5:58. Kim and I stayed with Nancy for a time before Kim left me alone with her. I'm not sure how long I stayed with her but I remember it being long enough, and that no one interrupted us. I used the time to thank Nancy for all she had done for me, to thank her for being with me, and for choosing to spend these last years of her life with me. I had told her these things while she was alive, but I could never ever tell her enough, or show her enough, that she meant the world to me. When I was ready to let go I heard the words she spoke over a year ago. Her last spoken words, "I love you."

We set the time of death at 5:56 as this was what we felt was right. Calls were made to the funeral home where I had made Nancy's arrangements and they came by to pick her up. But not before I was able wash her one more time, making sure that everyone would know how clean and proper she was.

I chose the funeral home I did because I toured it when I was becoming a volunteer at The WARM Place. One of the men who worked at the funeral home also volunteered at The WARM Place, on the same night I did. Had I thought of it I would have requested he be with the team that picked her up. As it turned out someone had taken care of that for me. He was the one who rang my doorbell. As we saw each other we embraced. He said, "I knew your wife was sick but I never dreamed I'd be picking her up."

I told him, "I didn't know either. But I'm so glad it's you." I assisted them, and watched as they took her out to the white van.

"I'll make sure we take good care of her," he said, as we embraced a final time. Then I watched them drive off.

I texted Nancy's brother Mike, and Nancy's friends Beth and Kerry, and my sister El, they would notify everyone else for me. I figured no one would call me that night; at least that's what I hoped.

After hospice left I finally got to experience the full weight of an empty house. I wasn't sure what to do. I knew I should rest but my head was swimming, and my heart was so full I had no idea what I was feeling. I knew the weight of the finality of what I had just experienced was beyond my ability to process, and at the same time there was a sense of relief that my Beloved Nancy was out of pain. I knew my pain would come soon enough.

Chapter 22

EVENING–SEPTEMBER 22, 2013

The one thing we held sacred those last weeks was expressing our emotions. We expressed them openly with each other. Complete honesty was the rule, no exemptions. Holding anything back was, to us, being dishonest. Honesty was the foundation of our relationship. I trusted that in some way that can't be explained that she would help me.

It's funny how we spend so much time reliving our past. I lay in our bed now and I look out the same two windows that Nancy looked through the last five weeks of her life, and I wonder how she saw life through these windows. Were the birds more precious, was she lost in different thoughts of the past, or of what she lost, not paying attention to the birds at all. Of course there was the routine of the day, with bathing and medications and the cats needing attention. I also read to her for as long as my voice would hold up. And friends would visit every few days. But even with all this seeming activity, there was still a lot of time with nothing going on but she and I sitting together.

For me, time was important, but Nancy was the one who was precious. I knew she would end too soon. I held onto each moment with her as if my holding could keep her from slipping away. But no matter how tight I grasped or how hard I concentrated she continued slowly leaving this life behind. Each moment I watched her, I was losing a little more of the most precious thing in my life.

With all we talked about there are still things I would have liked to ask: What was it that was most important to her those last days? Did she look at all the life around her and think, "This will all continue after I'm gone as if I had never been here." "Who will I see on the other side of the veil?" "I can't wait for the pain to leave and experience the Love that I know I am." It never entered my mind that her thoughts might be about me.

I never asked those things. All I could concern myself with was her comfort in this world. This is where I wanted her to stay. Now she is gone. All that is left for me is to rest in the knowledge that it is her turn to take care of me.

Just as those who have gone before become the teachers that help guide and direct us so that we may have an easier way, I asked Nancy to help me as I moved from the life we shared to a new life. She always said, no matter how good things are they can always be better. I could not imagine better than Nancy but I knew in my heart she was in a better space than she was with me, and I knew that she would want the same for me here, as soon as I am willing to accept it. In that thought I find some peace.

Though I cannot see her, or physically feel her touch, or hear her measured breathing, though I can no longer lay my head on her chest, or hear the beat of her heart, I know she is with me tonight. I feel her as strongly as I ever have. I welcome her in my thoughts. There are no regrets, only appreciation for all she gave to me. The most precious gift I could ever ask for; time with the one I love most.

I remember when my grandmother died. She had been married to my grandfather for fifty-nine years. After the funeral and family gathering were done, it was just my grandfather and I sitting alone on the porch. He gave me a sad smile and said, "I told her everything I wanted her to know, and she did the same for me. We left nothing unsaid and nothing undone. I guess there's not much more I could ask for."

Nancy and I were blessed to have shared the same type of relationship. We were complete at the end. I knew there was nothing more I could have asked of her that she could have given me. I knew she gave me more that I asked. All that was left was what do I do now? Luckily Nancy had left me a list of instructions.

I now have time. I can do whatever I want whenever I want. I spent some of the day putting away the things that are no longer necessary. Suction machines, cannula cleaning kits, emesis basins, and Nancy's food. I marvel as I walk around and look at all that I have created to make life easier for her.

It starts in the room with the special memory foam pillows that we bought so she could rest easier. I don't have to look far to see the machine that sends an electrical impulse to the cells to promote healing and ease pain. I see the rolling cart that was purchased and built to make it easier to keep all the stuff for cleaning and caring for the cannula. I see the table I set up in the bedroom to pay bills on so I wouldn't have to be away from her. In the bathroom are many bottles of oils and herbs and holistic remedies to help keep the effects of the tumors at bay. I see the microphone stand I used to hold up the attachment I made that would hold a feeding tube syringe so she could gravity feed, into the tube.

When she did this the food entered her stomach slowly. Pushing all the food in at once with the syringe made her nauseous. I will find the most things in the kitchen. Shelves full of food and food supplements along with homeopathic remedies and fiber. In the spare bedroom will be shelves of medical supplies like feeding syringes cannula cleaning kits, inner cannulas, drain sponges, spare basins, pads, cleaning supplies, hydrogen peroxide, and much, much more.

All of the full boxes have been donated to hospice. But there will be things I keep, like the water filtration system that reintroduces minerals into the water, the air filtration system for the whole house, and many other items. No expense was spared. No effort was spared. With all of this, it wasn't enough to heal her. I think, if only I had done more. Yet I have no clue what else I could have done.

It's the next day and I have slept for a total of five hours in the last two nights, but I can't sleep. It's still pretty early, and I have no idea what to do. I can do anything, but I don't know what. I called Mike.

"Mike," I say, "for the first time in almost a year I'm free to do whatever I want and I don't know what to do."

Mike said, "Just remember what Nancy would have wanted

for you. She would have wanted for you to move on when you could."

Mike's words were simple and accurate. They were also the truth. It was what Nancy wanted.

"Thanks Mike, I appreciate your words."

"So what are going to do bro?"

"I'm going to get something to eat and take it home."

"If you need to talk just give me a call."

"I will, I promise."

I hung up and went to a local restaurant and ordered a meal to go. It wasn't much, but it was a start. And in some ways it was monumental. It was only something I could have done by being reminded of Nancy's words.

"Things can always be better."

Chapter 23

SAYING GOODBYE–2013

I still had not really said goodbye to Nancy; though I believed I had. Everything that needed to be done for the service was in front of me. It was a lot like working with the doctors. I set appointments, made arrangements, decided what was needed, and knew what Nancy wanted ahead of time so I could tell others for her. Except for last night when I called Mike, it was almost like she was still here.

The funeral home called me the next day and asked me several questions; one, did I want to view Nancy before the cremation, two, how many copies of the death certificate did I want, and three, what information did I want in the obituary. I also needed to come down there and pick out an urn. At first I said no to the viewing as I knew no one would want to see her like she was, but a few hours later I asked if I could see her the next day, in the morning, since the cremation was scheduled in the evening. They said that would be fine.

The next day, I went to see Nancy for the last time. After arriving at the funeral home I was directed to a viewing room. The attendant did not go in with me but he did tell me to take all the time I needed. They had a chair set up in front of her and had her sitting up at almost the same angle as at home. She was not embalmed so she looked very natural and at peace. She was covered with a grandmother-style blanket up to her neck–the kind of blanket you find in a chest in the attic. It looked like it would have kept her warm. The breathing tube had been removed from her throat here at the house at my request before they took her, so you could see the small hole in her throat that had kept her alive for the past year and three months.

I spent a few moments just looking at her, so still now but with so much behind her. Then I spoke to her.

"Nancy, it has been such a privilege to be a part of your life. I've experienced more in our time together than I ever could have imagined. We have done more together than my father and mother and both of their parents combined. And the impact we have made on the lives of others will be felt for generations to come. It has been an honor to serve you, to care for you, and to call you my wife. Please visit me often. You will be in my thoughts as long as I have breath in me."

Then, as I had so many times at home over the last seven years, I kissed her forehead, and left the room. Outside, the attendant asked if there was anything else they could do. I shook my head no, and thanked them. I had an appointment later that day to pick out the urn. It would be stone and have her name on the top. I could pick it up with her cremains inside in a couple of days to bring her home. I returned to the car. I needed to figure out what was next.

We had decided on a memorial service at the church we attended. It would be in three days, which was six days after her death. Nancy gave me no indication of what music to play other than "Amazing Grace." I asked our friend Janis to sing it, but she was so consumed with grief she felt sure it would be too much. She did get us another singer, and I was pleased with her efforts.

I went through the pictures we had at home of Nancy as a child through adulthood. Especially those that showed the exciting life she lived. She had traveled around the world, around the U.S. and studied many different cultures and religions. There were plenty of photos to choose from. The last thing was to choose the background music for the photo show. I picked three songs that celebrated life and love. One of which sang about conveying love with no words. Everything was prepared in the end and all that was left was to get her ashes home.

Before Nancy left we discussed how she would take care of me after she moved on. We also talked about communication. I wanted to know that she was talking to me. I believed it would be through intuition. I knew passwords were out of the question, so I asked her to contact me in a way that would be unmistakable. In other words, I would know beyond a shadow of a doubt that it was her guiding me. Nothing startling had come to me since her death until after I picked up her cremains, which were safely in the urn.

As I held the urn containing Nancy's cremains I felt her presence as strongly as ever and she was telling me what to do so I would know she was communicating with me. The feeling was overwhelming, and I had no doubt this was Nancy's way of letting everyone know she was okay and would be looking over not only me, but her closest friends as well. The trouble was, if I did what she asked and others thought that this was not the case, it would cast a very bad light on me.

After much deliberation I returned home. It was time to trust that Nancy was indeed speaking to me. I went to the closet and opened a box. It contained the object I would need to carry out the task I had been instructed to do. I removed the Hat of Hats from the box and placed it on top of the urn. Looking at it I thought, "This is just what Nancy would do."

I then took a picture of it with my phone, and I texted the photo to those in the club and waited. The two possible responses would be that yes she's communicating with you, or the response might be something that involved words like vulgar, or inappropriate, or even something so bad that the *National Enquirer* wouldn't print it. I could not imagine the consequences of what I was about to do, but I trusted the overwhelming feeling that Nancy was fulfilling her promise. Within minutes I started to receive a reply to what I had sent. I received numerous texts, and calls telling me that it was so nice that Nancy was talking to me.

Others may think differently, and perhaps they are right. For me, the complete belief and faith in the guidance of those who have gone before, has always provided me with the confidence and initiative I needed to overcome life's greatest obstacles.

As the memorial approached and things started to be put into place I let people know that I would not be speaking at the service. I have always felt that these gatherings were more about others saying goodbye then for those closest to the deceased that had watched them perish. Still these things are desirable and help everyone to move on. What I wanted most out of the gathering was to meet with Nancy's closest friends at a local restaurant and talk about their memories of her. Doing this I knew we would all feel Nancy's presence and her pleasure at being honored in a true celebration of her companionship with us all.

On the day of the service things went as well as can be expected. There were lots of hugs and lots of tears. Stories were shared and songs were sung. We prayed and each in our own way said goodbye. For most, the pain would subside within a few days and things would begin to get back to normal. This is the way of things. We remember, but we move on. At least most will.

I have been to a lot of these services over the years, and lost many people close to me. I have always been one of the ones that can easily go on. It would turn out that this time would be different.

About thirty minutes after the service ended people were starting to filter out. I received about a dozen invitations to eat and took a raincheck on many of them, while politely turning down the rest. There were still some things that Nancy had asked me to do.

Arrangements were made so that after the service I would meet six of Nancy's friends at a nearby restaurant. As a surprise to them I would bring the Hat of Hats. Nancy and I had talked about the hat before her death to decide who would be its keeper. We had decided it would be Kerry. She was the one who was always there for us. She was also one of the original four who had their picture taken with the sombrero. We figured it would mean the most to her, and that's what it was all about.

When I arrived at the restaurant, we arranged a table for all of us to sit down and we ordered a round of beverages and some light snacks. We then began to talk about our Nancy and how we would miss her. I then pulled out the bag I had carried in and removed the Hat of Hats. I let the ladies know how much it meant to Nancy that they all came to the house to put it on and have their picture taken with it. Then I gave it to Kerry.

"Nancy and I talked about it, and we decided that it was not appropriate for me to keep the Hat of Hats. We both decided it should be Kerry that keeps it." I turned to Kerry and asked, "Will you accept responsibility for keeping the Hat of Hats safe from harm until such time as it becomes necessary to pass it on, or throw it out with the trash?"

"I will," said Kerry, "gladly. But I think you should also have a picture with the hat David."

With that I put it on and had my picture taken, so that I too could be immortalized as a wearer of the Hat of Hats.

I told them how Nancy and I never really talked about her past, but she had mentioned that it had been somewhat rambunctious.

Kerry started with, "Well she was a very good pool player. I remember one night she got pulled out of a pool hall by her hair for hustling this girl who was a lot bigger than her."

Kim said, "Yeah, that happened more than once. We all had some wild parties."

The stories went on and on and we laughed till we cried. These were things I never knew about Nancy, but it gave me solace that her life was fuller than I ever imagined. Then came the time I dreaded. There were flights to catch, and homes to return to, and let's face it, these ladies had put their lives on hold for this chance to say goodbye, but needed to get back to daily living. We hugged, we waved, and we went to our cars, and went home.

That was the beginning of an emptiness I had never before experienced. It was unexpected. I had a trip to plan and I had an ordination to attend. This should not be a time for loneliness, but it was. It was Nancy who always planned the trips. It was Nancy who made the arrangements. All I ever did was bring out suitcases and pack the car. I had to make this trip on my own, a trip that she inspired.

Some would say she would be with me on this trip. Of course I would agree with them, but this is not the way I wanted her with me. I wanted to be able to see her in the seat next to me. I wanted her to be telling me what was next because she planned it so well that she left very little to chance. And more than anything else, I wanted to hear her say, "I love you Honey Bunny."

When I got home I spent the evening getting ready, packing,

preparing food for the trip, and getting the map all set up. For the first time in the last seven years, I was preparing for a trip alone; there was nothing for me to do for Nancy. I found it strange. I was the only person I didn't know how to take care of. I was lost, and without a clear direction as to who I was, so I laid down where Nancy had spent her last days and I held the urn that now held all that was left of her physical being. I relaxed into sleep, hoping she could send me the guidance I needed to take the next step.

Chapter 24

THE BEGINNING–OCTOBER 2013

The list Nancy left was to let me know how to proceed. On it was a list of suggestions to try after she was gone. Things like; transfer money out my accounts as soon as you can and go on a little vacation, at three months you should see if you can get rid of my clothes if you haven't already, at six months if you haven't already, you should get out and go dancing. At the end of the list, was a letter she left, "Whenever you feel like you can, read this," she wrote. I didn't know what was in it, so I decided to wait till I got through the end of the list. The list was for me to heal and move on. She was teaching me how to let go of the past and pack for a new life as soon as I was ready to accept it.

I woke up the next morning at five. It had been about three weeks since Nancy's death. I was on my way to Canada for my ordination. I had a life purpose, an aim, a destination, but I had no idea how I was going to realize them; and really I just wanted my old ones back. Each moment seemed to stretch into an hour. It was like all the time that had moved so fast the last two months, was now slowing down to balance itself out. I realized that time going too fast or too slow, was about attachment to the past or the future. If I could just be in the moment it might be easier, so I asked myself, "where am I right now?"

In the moment I was missing Nancy.

Usually on a long drive I would find the first few hours would go quickly. I would be excited about the beginning of the journey and looking forward to getting to the first stop. I might make a call, but I was more likely to turn off the radio and just sit in silence. When I tried this, the silence was deafening. My mind screamed and my heart ached. It felt like I was in someone else's skin; like I was living a life that no longer belonged to me. I gave it to Nancy long ago, and I wasn't ready to take it back. I decided to make a call. The first was to my friend George.

"What's up Davo?" he asked, as he answered.

"I'm on my way to Canada for the ordination."

"That's a long drive. Where in Canada?"

"It's a small town called Elora, it's near Toronto."

"How long will you be gone?"

"About two weeks. After the ordination I'll be heading back to the states and going to visit my family in New Hampshire, then going to Connecticut to see some friends."

"Sounds like a great trip. How are you holding up, you sound like shit?"

"Well that's how I feel so I guess I should sound like that."

"You took good care of Nancy for a long time Davo, It's going to take a while to get over that. You don't need to go back to work right away do you?"

"We saved up so I could take some time off, so no, I don't have to go back to work."

"Well if I were you I'd take some time and just relax as best you can for a while. You're smart, you'll figure things out. Just remember that Nancy wanted you to be happy."

I thought about saying, "if she really wanted that she could have stuck around," but I knew it wasn't the truth.

"Well I'm in the St. Louis area and I need to negotiate the highway system. I'll talk to you later okay."

"Take care Davo."

With that we hung up. I knew it would be hard for my friends to talk to me. I should have spared him the awkwardness of the call, but there was something I needed and I knew it was out there somewhere, I just wasn't sure who to contact or how to get the information.

Once I got on Highway 70 the phone rang. It was a friend from church, named Betty. Betty and I had been friends for a long time. She had been supportive of Nancy and me, and helped us through the years with deepening our relationship. She asked how things were going and I explained my current feelings about the trip. Somehow we got to talking about some of the things that Nancy and I held as sacred during our years together. How being honest with each other, and taking each other's feelings into consideration were so important.

These were things that should be important in all relationships, yet we embraced these principles at a depth seldom experienced by others. Sharing information, no matter how vulnerable it made us was encouraged. The things we revealed to one another were done with the condition that it would never be used as leverage. We kept each other safe. From the time we were married, we would never look at each other in fear. We had developed closeness, a trust that was rare, that was inspired by both our pasts and her condition. Our faith in each other was virtually indestructible.

As I finished my long speech I remembered that Betty knew all of this, but she was kind. She said, "David, the things you went through were amazing, and everyone could see the depth of the relationship you shared with Nancy. Have you considered teaching this? Perhaps writing about it, or even doing classes?"

"Not really, but I did plan on writing a book on our time together."

"Information on what you've done needs to be made public. We all need to be lifted, to be brave enough to share what's in our hearts without the fear of having our innermost thoughts used against us."

"I'll give this some thought, and get back to you. You know I do feel a lot better having talked about this. Thanks so much."

"You're welcome David. Have the best time you can up in Canada."

After we hung up I found the drive to be more like the ones I was used to. I could feel Nancy beside me, and I spoke with her of my thoughts on what Betty and I had talked about. I spent my whole life talking about things that I never followed through with. I always wanted to write a book and even started one back in the nineties. I got about sixteen pages in and never picked it up again. My track record was terrible, but then again, I never had a relationship like the one with Nancy, and the one thing I did know for sure was that quitting before I even started would be a sure way of achieving failure.

I first started keeping a journal after our second year of marriage. It started out as a gratitude journal then it turned into a written account of the things we had done to cure the cancer. Then it I started to document what we were thinking about all the time, followed by what was happening in our lives in relation to what we were thinking about. Although the first journal was abstract at best, when I would read it I found myself remembering the details of what happened at that time in our lives. After I realized that, I kept an account of our daily events and how we felt about them. It made a difference to both of us.

At the end of the first year Nancy asked to read my journal. I handed it to her and let her see all that went on in our lives, in my head, and in my heart. She did not judge me on anything I wrote, and even expressed appreciation of what I was doing. For the rest of her life, at the end of each year she would ask to read my journal. I believe by allowing this she could see my fears about her dying while I was away on a retreat; she could understand how terrified I was at Delicate Arch in Utah; she could know that my greatest fear was not my death, but hers. She never tried to fix me after reading about these fears. She accepted that we both had fears and by my sharing mine it was easier for her to share as well. We accepted each other as we were.

I began to understand what Betty was talking about. The first night on the road I wrote on a blank page in big bold letters, "A Seven Year Lifetime." It was my way of making a commitment. This commitment was not about a cancer patient, it wasn't about being a caregiver; it was about being a partner. In my case, cancer didn't happen to my life. I chose it, because it came with the one I loved most. And while I may have lost Nancy, she would always be a part of who I am, today, and from now on.

The next morning I made the final hour drive to the Canadian border and passed through the countryside toward my destination, Elora.

It was obvious to me that my old life was over. Nancy wasn't the only one who left, I left too, but it felt like I had been thrown out. I gave Nancy so much space in my life, now it was vacant; even this trip had emptiness about it because I felt empty without her. Every event, every experience I tried to use to fill the space previously reserved for her evaporated into meaninglessness. There was no place to hide because I had taken down my walls of refuge to build my relationship with her. I hoped this trip would give life some meaning with the discovery of the book and my ordination, but up until now no matter how I tried to connect with the world, there was just emptiness. This is how I felt as drove my car into the gravel parking lot at my destination.

There is a small divinely inspired bed and breakfast called Drew House where the retreat and ordination would take place. Drew House was only available to those on a Spiritual Journey as a place of rest and spiritual rejuvenation. It was quiet and old with shared bathrooms and old squeaky wooden floors and smooth plaster walls. The owner is Roger Dufau, one of the most deeply spiritual men I have met. He expressed his love of God through his preparing and cooking of food. I called him the patron saint of edibles.

I met his wife Kathleen at check-in and was shown to my room. It was huge with a big wide double-hung window that over looked the garden. It was magnificent. The king-size bed had a beautiful handmade quilt on it that looked so welcoming it was all I could do not to jump in and take a nap. She told me the location of the dining area where we would all meet for meals, and where the garden was that I could see from my window. I was free to walk the grounds at any time but should be respectful of the other guest during quiet hours. She left me to unpack and I felt the onset of a peace I had not known since before Nancy's death. I welcomed it, as I walked outside to sit in the garden.

There were thirteen of us for the retreat and there would be about eleven, including myself who would attend the ordination. As these retreats are deeply personal and cannot be explained without possibly revealing some personal communication I will not go into the events of the days that followed, except to say that the comfort that Nancy's friends, family, and myself gave to Nancy during her final days would have been rivaled by the support I felt from these spiritual beings that worked with me over that weekend. Walls were taken down and the intimacy I had shared with my beloved Nancy was the conscious choice of our experience during the retreat, for the entire time. Everything was shared; including our mealtime. I found that the emptiness could be filled, that it was possible to have friends who could share life on a level congruent with my personal experience over the last seven years.

Mealtime at Drew House was when I thought most of Nancy. I decided that if I could remember her as I ate, that she could experience the same enjoyment I felt as I savored each dish that was being served.

Roger Dufau is a master chef. I do not believe it is possible to consume anything of his creation and not be in heaven. This was an experience I chose to believe I was sharing with Nancy because to exclude her would be the only thing that would have diminished the meals. I imagined her tasting everything as I did. I could see the pleasure in her face, as she urged me have some more of the potatoes, or take another sip of the coffee made fresh from the press. I could feel her satisfaction that I would include her in this event, even if she could not physically be here.

I told my fellow diners, "This must be what love taste like."

They shook their heads in agreement not wishing to talk with their mouths full. Every meal was planned out by getting local fresh foods at their peak of flavor. I felt truly blessed to be here.

By the time the stole was placed around my neck at the conclusion of the ordination ceremony, I felt whole mentally, physically, and spiritually. I believed I could live again; not without Nancy, but with her in a new relationship; one that did not consume me, but fueled my desire to grow and contribute to all I would come in contact with. I also knew someday I could have someone else in my life as Nancy had suggested, and I knew my work here was not finished, in many ways it was just beginning.

> *"**We** shall not cease from exploration, and the end of all our exploring will be to arrive where we started, and know the place for the first time."*

T.S. Eliot wrote this many years before my experience, but it played over and over in my head as I made my way back into the journey of my lifetime, a lifetime that was perhaps ending, but also beginning anew.

Chapter 25

A YEAR LATER–2014

By the time I was in my teens I had lost my mother, older brother, two great grandparents, several uncles, and a classmate. With these as my most prominent experiences I could honestly say I knew more about death than life. Today, I know about both.

All our stories end in death, mine will too. I look around at what I wanted to keep. Each picture has a story behind it; each object that I kept had some important memory associated with it. When my life ends these objects will be forgotten or discarded and new lives will inhabit the space that I once called home. My story, which was so important to me, will be lost within a generation of my passing, and the story of those who touched my life will go with me. This happens every day, somehow I never noticed until now. I think about this and find it is okay. I'll know the difference I made.

I pull out the list. It's completed now. I've even read the letter. It's kind of like graduating from a specialty school. Just because you've passed all the tests, it doesn't mean you're an expert, or even qualified to do what your diploma says you can do. That's how I feel now. I have done what was expected of me, but I don't know what to expect from myself. There are parts of me that still feel lost, so I go back to the beginning, to see if I retrace my steps, I can find my way back to who I am now.

A parting letter from Nancy:

Dear David,

Thank you for caring for me and seeing me as someone worthy of love and affection, even when I could no longer believe it. You always thought ahead to anticipate what the needs would be, and then you would tap into your creative mind and have what I needed all put together.

Thank you for your infinite supply of energy. There were very few times I saw you falter, and even then you rebounded quickly. I felt so loved and I meant it when I said you were the best decision I ever made.

I want you to be happy. Follow your heart to your greatest good, that's what brought you to me! You have always gone full out, while I hesitated, and now look where you are. Don't hold back now. Find the "one" and the "path" that brings you bliss. You and I know there is always "One" in every moment.

Your Honey Bunny
P.S. Things can always be better

David's parting letter written eight months after Nancy's death.

Dear Nancy,

Thank you so much for choosing me to care for you. If you were choosing to leave, I hope I offered all the support you required. I hope I loved you enough, at least with my heart. I hope I conveyed to you that you were the most important person in the world to me, and that there was no sacrifice too great. Mostly I hope I did it in a way that would not make you feel guilty or at fault. We both chose our challenges and each other. You gave me everything I wanted most: time and unconditional love.You gave me words, and when the words left you, you gave me more than words with a single loving expression. I could feel the intention in every touch from you, and when you were too weak to reach for me, you touched me with your eyes. Just holding your hand or rubbing your feet I could see you expressing your love and appreciation. Every day you let me know that you loved me a thousand times. You expressed the love of a lifetime to me every day, for the Seven Years we shared together.... Love, David

I received an email today. It is the one-year anniversary of Nancy's death. The email asked one question. The one question that those who have lost a loved one, get sick of hearing within minutes of the loss, because we have been hearing it for far too long already.

Dear David, how are you doing?

How am I doing? This is a question for the ages, and one that is well asked on this day. I had planned on being at the lake today, but instead I will be removing countertops and the backsplash at the house here. The new counter will be installed tomorrow.

Of course that's not how I'm doing, that's what I'm doing. How am I doing? I don't know yet. I got to bed late last night and got up a little late too, I'm reliving her last hours and it started last night. It continues now. One year ago, I would be calling hospice at ten a.m. to set up 24-hour care. They would arrive about an hour later and we would go over paperwork. Our friend Kim would come by around five p.m., and Nancy would be gone at 5:56 p.m. Yes I have relived this day before and it will always be fresh in my memory, and like most memories, it will always end the same.

I'm avoiding the question. How am I doing? How am I doing? I'm sad. I miss her presence. I feel like I'm losing her all over again..... Sometimes it hurts, but it hurts more to push her away. The sorrow squeezes my chest so that I can hardly breathe. That's okay, by tomorrow I'll realize she's always here, behind the scenes helping me for as long as I need; for as many times as it takes, until I remember..... There is no death for her experience, only for me, and those left behind. Then the same memory that took my breath will offer expansion, and I will remember how grateful I am to have known her, and how grateful I am to have shared a lifetime with her. I will once again remember what she wanted for me.

This alone might be enough for me to feel better. It should be. Yet there is always some hidden part that wonders why she left, or why I couldn't save her life. There will be no room for logic in this line of thinking, although I try to reason that it was not up to me. I did all that I could.

Still, I feel I'm missing something. It's like I'm trying to find my car in a crowded parking lot by standing on the roof of the car I'm looking for. All I need to do is look down to know what I'm looking for is here where I am. So I metaphorically look down, and see what I have missed all along. The car and the answer I seek are here at my feet. There is nowhere to look other than right here.

I go into the bedroom, and lay on the bed where she spent her last moments. Tears once again fill my eyes. I welcome them. I understand. I feel the realization of what she's been telling me all along; finally and completely. I was not sent here to save her... She was sent to save me.

Epilogue

At the end, Nancy suffered, and perhaps you could say I did also, but there was so much more. It didn't matter. Those last months were the most precious of the multitude of moments we spent together throughout our relationship, and perhaps throughout our entire lives. During that time most of our attention was on just being together. Never before in our lives had we cherished each other's company so much. Nothing needed to be said, no plans needed to be made, and there was no problem that could take our attention away from each other.

Perhaps for the first time in both our lives we were truly so close that not only was there no feeling of separation, there was no fear of the future. The present was too big to let anything else in. The memory of that time forever nourishes my spirit, and has enabled me to move forward in my life. This was a gift we gave to each other freely, with no expectation or proof needed from one another. It was the single most important thing in helping me to move on.

Our desire was to in some small way contribute to others who may need to see that this is possible. And also to show those who have good health and a promising life ahead of them that openness and honesty form the mortar for a strong foundation that can bring you closer than a thousand gifts, love letters, or houses all over the world. It frees you to live a life without restriction. Only when you have nothing to hide are you truly free. A true unity can only be accomplished when both give freely with their hearts completely open. If you think the only way to achieve this is to be facing death, I have news for you; you are facing death until you are willing to turn around and face life.

This book was not written as a tribute to Nancy or me: It will not make it romantic or okay to have cancer or any debilitating condition, nor heroic to be the caregiver of such a patient. It was written as a statement that although death is the ending of our journey here on earth, it is also part of continuing life both here and in the hereafter. It was written as a demonstration of how pure unconditional unbound love, can remove every distraction, and allow us to live an exceptionally full life in whatever time we have left here on earth.

In the end it will make no difference if anyone remembers me in the years after my death, or even Nancy for that matter. What will matter is that others can go through an experience like Nancy and I, and find that love is never lost. It will continue beyond the time I felt was so important, and beyond the space that we ourselves occupy, and though the love may be nameless it can touch the lives of all who desire it.

I offer blessings from Nancy and me, for the best life possible; a life of love, laughter, adventure, joy, and even a little sadness. Most of all we wish you a life of companionship, and deep connection purified with honest, open hearts. This will carry and support you throughout your journey, both in life and in death, and even into the next lifetime.

Many who have helped with this book have asked about the list. They wonder if this magical list could help them in some way move past a loss or some tragedy in their lives. Nancy and I knew each other as completely in seven years as my grandparents, (it took them almost sixty years). She made the list because she knew me. She gave it to me because she trusted me to accept it in the manner in which it was given. I accepted it because I knew when she was gone, I would be lost. It was her way of reminding me who I was before I became a fulltime caregiver.

If you want to know what should be on your list, talk to the one you most deeply trust. Share with them your deepest darkest secrets. Listen to their secrets as well. Love each other without any judgment. Only then will you be able to receive the list made just for you. You will then be responsible for completing it on your own. If the person you loved and trusted most has passed or chose to leave in some other way, go inside your heart. You will find them there waiting, with white paper, and a blue pen.

LIST SUGGESTIONS

Before list, for every day of your life:

1. Develop lifelong friendships; they can save your life.

2. Let others know your after-death wishes.

3. Live until you die. No Excuses.

4. Be honest, secrets are the shovels that dig the chasms of separation.

5. Be present no matter how much it might hurt.

6. Love, forgive, listen, hold hands, and spend as much time as you can, looking into one another's eyes.

After death list for those left behind:

7. Remember you are never alone.

8. Know that True Love is without condition, it last forever.

9. Be grateful; there is always something to be grateful for.

If you go to, www.sevenyearlifetime.com you will find information on programs, and workbooks available to assist, or mentor you in your journey through life and death, as well as links to organizations that have proven helpful.

CPSIA information can be obtained
at www.ICGtesting.com
Printed in the USA
LVOW03s0301130318
569660LV00002B/688/P

9 781633 932920